A DAY on the FARM

Finding Hope in a Hopeless Situation

ALLISON ROMNEY

Copyright © 2016 Allison Romney.

Llama photo credit: Blue Moon Studio

All rights reserved. No part of this book may be used or reproduced by any means, graphic, electronic, or mechanical, including photocopying, recording, taping or by any information storage retrieval system without the written permission of the author except in the case of brief quotations embodied in critical articles and reviews.

This book is a work of non-fiction. Unless otherwise noted, the author and the publisher make no explicit guarantees as to the accuracy of the information contained in this book and in some cases, names of people and places have been altered to protect their privacy.

WestBow Press books may be ordered through booksellers or by contacting:

WestBow Press
A Division of Thomas Nelson & Zondervan
1663 Liberty Drive
Bloomington, IN 47403
www.westbowpress.com
1 (866) 928-1240

Because of the dynamic nature of the Internet, any web addresses or links contained in this book may have changed since publication and may no longer be valid. The views expressed in this work are solely those of the author and do not necessarily reflect the views of the publisher, and the publisher hereby disclaims any responsibility for them.

Any people depicted in stock imagery provided by Thinkstock are models, and such images are being used for illustrative purposes only.
Certain stock imagery © Thinkstock.

ISBN: 978-1-5127-3844-5 (sc)
ISBN: 978-1-5127-3845-2 (hc)
ISBN: 978-1-5127-3843-8 (e)

Library of Congress Control Number: 2016906168

Print information available on the last page.

WestBow Press rev. date: 04/21/2016

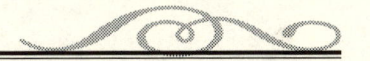

For my beautiful children and all the amazing people who came to help on the farm

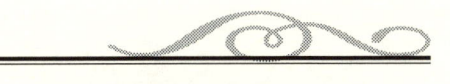

CONTENTS

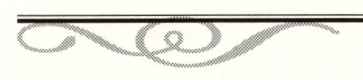

Prologue		ix
Chapter 1	Cold, Dark Days	1
Chapter 2	My New Friend, Bob	6
Chapter 3	The Shortest Month	13
Chapter 4	Lambing	17
Chapter 5	Spring Arrives	28
Chapter 6	New Life, New Hope	35
Chapter 7	The Garden	46
Chapter 8	Summer Visitors	51
Chapter 9	The Fall	60
Chapter 10	Spiritual Warfare	78
Chapter 11	Off to Market	83
Chapter 12	Farm Lessons	88
Chapter 13	The Biggest Lesson	93
Chapter 14	Forgiveness and Healing	98
Epilogue		101

PROLOGUE

Years ago, my coworkers and I decided to adopt a needy family at Christmas. We selected a single mother with two young children from the many needy families wanting help. Their long wish list included clothes and toys for the kids and household furnishings for their rented flat. But their single most important need seemed to be a working refrigerator. We brainstormed ideas on how to cross as many items off their list as possible, given our limited budgets and meager salaries. Somebody suggested contacting businesses that might be willing to help. We were elated when a local appliance dealer offered to donate a new refrigerator. But we had to find a way to move it.

As weeks went on, we scoured newspaper ads for sales on toys and clothes for the kids. Gradually, we purchased and wrapped most of the items for the children but still struggled to find a way to move the refrigerator. A few days before we planned to deliver the gifts, somebody found a pick-up truck big enough to haul the fridge and enough workers and a dolly to get it moved. We celebrated God's timing.

On delivery day, I stayed behind at work to cover the phones while the rest of the group loaded up the presents, picked up the refrigerator, and headed out to brighten a family's Christmas. I eagerly waited for the group to return and share the joyous story. But when they returned, their faces showed only disappointment. "What happened?" I asked.

They explained that they'd driven up in the truck and carefully parked in between the snowbanks. The two kids came running onto the porch with no winter jackets, followed by their mother, who was smoking a cigarette. The kids ran around and misbehaved, totally ignored by Mom. My friends carried the large box of gifts into the living room, and the kids ripped the wrapping off and started playing with the toys. They unloaded the refrigerator and wheeled it into the kitchen. As they released the straps from the dolly and removed the tarp protecting the fridge, the mother exclaimed, "I didn't want a white refrigerator! I wanted an almond-colored one."

My coworkers couldn't believe the scene. Their disappointment stemmed from a reaction of complete ingratitude. Yet how many times do we look at God's tremendous blessings and dare to ask Him what He was thinking in giving us something that wasn't exactly what we wanted?

And so my journey began when God gave me a farm.

CHAPTER 1

Cold, Dark Days

On the coldest day in February, the reality of my situation hit me. I got up early, lingered over my morning coffee and oatmeal, and then started layering the clothes to go outside and do chores. First, I put on silk underwear and then cotton leggings and a bamboo turtleneck to absorb all the sweat from the hard physical labor I would soon endure. I kept telling myself this would be better than a workout at the gym. Two pairs of wool socks—very nice socks I'd hand-knit myself—covered my feet and lower legs, followed by snow pants and a fleece jacket. I put on my boots, which were rated to minus thirty degrees Fahrenheit. The top layer needed to be put on quickly so I would not overheat before heading out the door and into the frigid winter. The morning news had issued freeze flesh warnings due to a windchill of about minus forty degrees. Fortunately, I would be working among several outbuildings on the farm, and most of the time, I could avoid a direct blast of wind coming at me. So I only needed to be prepared for about fifteen to twenty degrees below zero. On went the alpaca hat, down ski jacket, leather gloves covered by wool mittens, and a wool scarf wrapped around my face and neck. I knew I wouldn't freeze, but I wondered how I could possibly move through the snow. I didn't have a choice. The animals had to be fed. Chores had to be done, and I was the only person around to do them.

When I opened the back door and felt the cold, it actually felt good. I prepared well and marched into the cold—my first day alone on the farm. When I opened the granary door to get the corn mixture for the pregnant ewes, I saw none mixed up. My heart sank. I needed to climb up the cold metal silo steps and into the corn bin to get the corn. I trudged through the snow, and that's when it hit me. I thought, *I have no job, no income, no husband, and nobody else living with me, but I have a farm—just me and God on this big old farm.* I wanted to cry so badly, but I had to hold in the tears for fear they would freeze on my face.

When I got to the silo, I noticed that all the metal steps were covered in ice. My boots gripped well, but the straight vertical ascent meant I had to carry a five-gallon bucket in my heavy winter clothes up three-inch steel rungs coated in ice. With each step I took, I prayed, "Keep me safe. Keep me safe. Keep me safe." When I reached the top, I pounded on the latches to loosen the ice, opened the hatch, and leaned inside. I scooped up a bucket of corn, held on for dear life, and closed the hatch. Each step on the way down, I prayed the same prayer. It had worked on the way up, so I figured it should be just as good on the way down. "Keep me safe, God. Keep me safe. Keep me safe." When my feet hit the ground, I breathed a huge sigh of relief and simply said, "Thank You, God."

I returned to the granary, out of the wind, and mixed the corn and feed pellets together. After I loaded up the buckets with the feed, I headed back out into the cold toward the sheep pens. The sheep started baaing as soon as they caught sight of me. This was the highlight of their day. I smiled as I climbed into the pens and jostled between the sheep. Their beauty struck me in the midst of an extremely cold morning. Their breath steamed the air, and some of the yearlings ran and jumped all the way to the feed trough. I worked quickly, checking them all over, peering through the tiny slit between my scarf and hat. They looked beautiful, wrapped in their natural wool coats.

I checked the barn to make sure everyone had come out to eat. While the sheep ate, I chipped the ice out of the watering tanks with a metal ice chipper. The ice chipper resembled a sharpened metal rectangle connected to a long handle, like a broom handle. Forceful thrusts onto the top of the ice barely made a dent. I pounded harder and harder. Finally, a slit broke open, and water gushed up, freezing as soon as it hit the air. Eventually, I created a hole about six inches wide with open water. Electric heaters kept the pipes from freezing inside the tanks, but the temperature of the surface water was no match for the winter air. I would have to break the ice open again later in the day.

Pitching hay into the feed bunks came next. Several large square bales had been left on the ground next to the pens. Each large bale weighed seven hundred to eight hundred pounds and provided enough hay for about a week. I couldn't grip the pitchfork with my wool mittens, so I removed them, leaving the leather gloves, and pitched several slabs of hay into the bunk as fast as I could. Within five minutes, I could no longer feel my fingers. They hurt so much that I wanted to cry. I held in the tears again, since they would only freeze on my face, and I ran to the nearest building with running water and a heater inside. I removed the leather gloves and shoved my hands inside my coat next to my belly. My fingers were practically frozen and hurt with the rush of heat. Then I cried. The tears flowed, and I cried out to God to give me the strength to finish the chores and protect my fingers from frostbite. When I could finally feel my fingers and wipe away the tears, I bundled back up and went back out to finish pitching the hay.

The cold pierced me, and I prayed again for strength. The words of the doxology popped into my head, and I started singing as loudly as I could inside my muffled wraps:

> Praise God from whom all blessings flow; praise Him all creatures here below.
>
> Praise Him above, ye heavenly hosts; praise Father, Son, and Holy Ghost.

It worked. The singing kept my mind off the cold and the physical pain it caused. As soon as the last of the hay landed in the bunk, I dropped the pitchfork and ran as fast as I could to the warm house. I stripped off the layers of clothes, took a hot shower, and thanked God that I had made it through the first hour of being a farmer.

In addition to caring for thirty-six ewes, eleven market lambs, a ram, a wether named Barney, nine alpacas, four llamas, and a bunch of farm cats, I now was also responsible for running a retail yarn store that offered products for sale from the farm, natural fiber yarns, and gifts. It was open to the public seven days a week, and it was up to me and one part-time worker to keep it going. That day, I was the only one on duty.

I trudged through the snow to the back entrance of the store, switched on the lights, turned up the heat, put the open sign out, and waited for customers. I wasn't disappointed that the day was a bit slow because of the cold weather. A few determined knitters made it in to pick out yarn for new projects, because as every knitter knows, neither wind nor rain nor sleet nor snow can prevent a knitter from getting new yarn.

In between customers, I pondered my situation. One year before, I'd been working as a stockbroker and managing $50–60 million in assets, depending on the market. I wore suits to my very own office, served hundreds of clients, and had an assistant to help me; when the sun set before the office closed at five o'clock, the sign above my door would automatically light up for all the folks to see as they drove by on the busy city street. One year before, I would come home from work to eat dinner with my husband, my high school sweetheart and the love of my life, and we would talk about his day on the farm. One year before, I was looking forward to my retirement from the world of investments within a few short months, when I would work alongside my husband and transition into our golden years on the farm that I had worked so hard to support financially. At that time, I had thought the hard work of helping people ride the stock market roller coaster would be over—that the days would be more enjoyable when I could just focus on knitting, gardening, and helping my husband with the animals when the chores required more than two hands. One year before, I was looking forward to a trip to Prague with my husband and a couple of friends, one last vacation to Europe before I retired. God knew the very different direction my life would take; I didn't have a clue.

CHAPTER 2

My New Friend, Bob

Drawing on years of corporate training and experience, I assessed my situation with SWOT. When faced with uncertainty, I typically had learned to identify strengths, weaknesses, opportunities, and threats. I certainly knew the weaknesses and threats—minimal farming experience, incredible emotional pain, mental and physical exhaustion from the unbearable workload, and lack of money. And the list grew longer. But I had to focus on finding the strengths and opportunities. I knew my faith in God was one of the few sure things I could count on to hold me together. I prayed for God to help me see what needed to be done and to send me help. He opened my eyes to see positive things in front of me and sent people to help me manage.

I first looked to Sophia, my only part-time store employee, who worked a few hours a month. I relied on Sophia as a strong Christian woman who kept her word, and I trusted her to keep confidences. She never let me down. She knew about all the dirt in my life.

A Day on the Farm

Sophia first entered my life years earlier when I desperately needed a cleaning lady for my house. I worked long hours as a stockbroker and lived with teenagers and a husband in a big, old farmhouse. Because of the kids' extensive involvement in school academics and sports, I knew the seasons by the sports they played. Girls' field hockey and boys' soccer started in late summer and fall; winter brought swimming, ski team, and wrestling; and spring ended the year with girls' soccer and boys' track and field. In between school, homework, and sports, the kids worked as lifeguards and swim instructors, and my son, Jim, played drums in a band. In addition to keeping schedules straight, attending as many home games and meets as possible, preparing healthy, home-cooked meals, and working more than a full-time job, I also chaperoned Jim when his band played in bars because he was underage. I never managed to find time to clean my house, nor did any of the other family members.

I tried to get references for cleaning help at Rotary meetings and by asking clients. If someone used a really good cleaning person, they guarded the contact information with their life. Eventually, somebody cracked and gave me a name. I called her, and she agreed to meet me at the house to look things over. I arranged my work schedule to be home in the middle of the day, but she never showed up. After several unsuccessful attempts to meet her, I moved on to another referral. My referral source forewarned me that the cleaning lady only had one eye and couldn't drive, but her eyesight didn't interfere with her cleaning skills. I lived in the country, miles from her home. When I called her, she agreed to give it a try and arranged for her husband to drop her off and pick her up. My flexibility in the days she cleaned was helpful, since nobody stayed in the house at all during the week days and she could work around her husband's schedule to get the cleaning done.

The first few cleaning days went well. Nothing beats walking in the door at the end of a long day to find everything spotless. My happiness didn't last long, though; I got home from work one day, and my one-eyed cleaning lady was still vacuuming upstairs. When I walked in the door, a large man peered up from the refrigerator and greeted me with an unusual question: "Where's your pop? You don't have anything good in here for me to drink. And you don't have any good snacks in the cupboards." Surprised, I asked who he was. It turned out that the chauffeur husband took up residence in my house for five hours while the cleaning took place and helped himself to whatever he chose. As hard as it was to let my one-eyed cleaning lady go, I felt I didn't have much of a choice. That's when Sophia entered the picture.

Sophia's friend cleaned for my mother-in-law, and though Sophia's friend personally couldn't take on my project, she knew that Sophia wanted some extra work. Sophia and her husband traveled as missionaries to Guatemala for several weeks at a time. As long as I didn't mind her periodic absences, she offered to clean my house as a part-time job. Sophia turned out to be very reliable. She came when she said she would, cleaned thoroughly, respected our home, and shared her faith with my teenage son. She offered more than what I ever hoped to hire.

As my kids grew and headed off to college, Sophia came to clean less frequently, but I looked forward to her visits more each time. When my husband started his farm business with the sheep and decided to open the yarn shop, Sophia came to the rescue. A few weeks before the store opening, I faced truckloads of yarn boxes sitting in a renovated farm building and wondered what we were thinking in this venture. After long hours at the office, I came home each night to meticulously enter inventory into the store computer and print out hundreds of price tags. Sophia begged us to let her help put the price tags on all the yarn. When I told her we couldn't afford to hire anyone for the store, she said, "I'm not asking to get paid. I'm volunteering to help you get started." Sophia spent hours putting price tags on yarn and even brought her daughter along to volunteer. So when the time eventually came to hire someone to help out, Sophia switched from cleaning my house to working in the store.

Sophia knew all the dirt. She didn't judge and offered support in any way she could. She kept me and my family in her prayers. She came to pray with me whenever I asked. Sophia also gave me one of her favorite Bible studies on the Holy Spirit. Being Lutheran, I didn't fully understand the power of the Holy Spirit, but I diligently delved into Scripture and learned that God was an even stronger force in my life than I thought. My prayer life strengthened, and miracles started happening.

The first little miracle arrived with a snowstorm. Along with the intense cold, midwestern winters can bring a lot of snow. Shortly after I found myself alone on the farm, a storm dumped about a foot of snow, and the howling winds moved it around into snowdrifts as high as eight feet. I contracted with a snow removal company to keep the store parking lot and entrance to the house open, but the hay buildings remained inaccessible. I got up even earlier than usual and started shoveling paths to walk between the buildings. I only had a few days until I needed to replenish the hay supply. In addition to the large rectangular bales that required a skid loader to move them, some small thirty- to thirty-five-pound bales remained in another building. I could easily carry a bale at a time, stopping every few feet to catch my breath. But the sheep needed six to eight bales twice a day, and just getting the food to them seemed daunting. I kept praying for help.

Shortly after the snow piled up, one of my long-time knitting friends brought her boyfriend to the store to talk with me. John retired from a career in road construction and almost lost his life in a skid loader accident. He knew a bit about my situation and wanted to help. He asked about equipment on the farm and if I knew how to use any of it. Honestly, I could see the inventory listing of the equipment, but I knew little else. My minimal interaction with the Bobcat 773 skid loader came the summer before when I needed to move some mulch for the garden. I figured out how to start it, and through trial and error, I maneuvered the levers to get the pile moved. Twenty minutes of experience didn't seem significant, but it was a start. I certainly wasn't afraid to learn more.

John offered to come the next morning for my first lesson. To my surprise, he spent most of the time talking about safety. I learned that the skid loader had a seat belt and how to adjust it. Seriously, I never expected any farm equipment to have a seat belt, and frankly, I hadn't noticed it under all the hay and garbage inside the cab. I also learned how to move around, especially in heavy winter outerwear, without falling and injuring myself. John explained, "You always need three points of contact." He continued, "You have two arms and two legs. Make sure that three of them always have contact with the equipment and you are only moving one limb at a time. You'll keep your balance and not kill yourself falling." I thought I had good balance from years of yoga classes. But I needed to stay healthy and couldn't risk a serious fall. He also insisted that I wear earplugs so I wouldn't go deaf over time. The most significant pointer he offered was that simply taking my hands off the controls would immediately stop the machine from doing whatever was happening at the time.

When I fully understood the safety measures, including checking around the machine for debris and hazards on the ground, John taught me how to properly start the Bobcat in cold weather. I knew how to plug in the extension cord to the heater for a few hours before starting it up, but I didn't know that I shouldn't turn the key in the ignition all the way until the code "Glo19" went to zero. Once the machine was running, John shouted, "Okay, good. Now throttle up."

I sat there, seat-belted in, with no clue what he was talking about. I turned the machine off and asked him, "What's a throttle?"

He didn't roll his eyes or laugh at me but patiently pointed to the large red lever at the right side of the seat and said, "When you want to go faster or need more power, like when you're lifting a large bucket of snow, you move it forward."

I started the Bobcat up again and cautiously plowed myself out of the machine shed. I practiced moving some snow and getting used to the bucket. I learned how to move the hydraulic levers to go forward and back, up and down, and tilt. Moving both levers forward at the same time moved the machine forward. The left joystick controlled

A Day on the Farm

raising and lowering the bucket, and the right joystick controlled the tilt of the bucket. If I moved either the left or right lever, the machine turned in that direction. I memorized little ditties, like "lefty lifts," which just meant that when I moved the left lever to the left, the bucket lifted up. It seems simple, but that has helped me out of a few jams along the way.

The lesson ended way too soon because I needed to get cleaned up and open the store. But I felt tremendous excitement and gratitude that God brought me someone to help who truly cared about my life and knew what I didn't yet understand. John had stayed to watch me as I learned how to move a few snowdrifts. But when I went to put the Bobcat back in the shed, he asked if I minded if he "stuck around a little bit longer to try a few things out." Of course, I didn't mind. John stopped in the store a while later, and I made him some fresh coffee. He offered to help with anything else that might come up and gave me his cell number. I humbly thanked him for his assistance, and I thanked God for the hope that John brought with him that day. I could handle moving the rest of the snow, and I could handle another snowstorm.

When I closed the store later that day, opened the back door, and went out to do the afternoon chores, I couldn't believe my eyes. All the snow was neatly piled up and moved out of the way. John had stayed to finish a job I never asked him to do out of the kindness of his heart and perhaps his sympathy toward my inexperience. He saved me hours and hours of work, and I remain incredibly grateful to someone I had just met.

John continued to help on the farm and provided more lessons with the skid loader. He showed me how to safely switch buckets, including where to store the accessories to get to them off and on easily, and he showed me how to safely stack and move eight-hundred-pound hay bales. My confidence increased each time I used the equipment. And I had a new friend, Bob the Bobcat skid loader. That year, Bob became a huge strength for me and my survival on the farm.

My new friend, Bob, helped me survive life on the farm.

CHAPTER 3

The Shortest Month

February contains the fewest days because we can't bear more freezing temperatures and growing piles of snow turned black from road dirt and grime. The weather becomes dreadful. Cars turn white from salted highways, and people get grumpy. When winter arrives, Christmas appears soon after, and celebrations carry us through many cold days and nights. By the end of winter, before the warmer days of spring arrive, everyone is just plain tired of it. Sometimes twenty-eight days can seem like an eternity. Throw in a leap year, and it's almost too much.

When the kids were younger and still in school, I rarely got away from home during the winter. But once they went off to college, my husband and I looked forward to traveling each February to someplace warm and relaxing. We wanted to thaw out, play, and return to the farm refreshed. Our first February trip happened just two years earlier when we spent a week on a tiny island in the Caribbean. Traveling to Anguilla took more than a day because we had to take a boat from St. Maarten to the island,

and no direct flights to St. Maarten departed from our closest airports. We chose to spend a day in New York, visiting the former World Trade Center and sitting in the audience for a taping of David Letterman's show, something I had on my bucket list for about twenty years.

We landed in St. Maarten in the morning, took a car to the boat ferry, processed through customs in Anguilla, and lay on the beach that afternoon. The next few days became a second honeymoon for us. We had privacy and were surrounded by the most beautiful scenery anyone could imagine. We had a small, private pool on our balcony, which overlooked palm trees and the ocean. We slept in each day, rode bicycles around the island, and went to as many different beaches as we could find. I took waterfront yoga classes, and at night, we enjoyed fresh seafood and reggae music. Sometimes we got lucky and found a beachfront restaurant with live music during the day.

My husband was my high school sweetheart, and I was lucky enough to end up married to him later in life. That week in Anguilla became one of the high points of our marriage; I felt romance and connection in a way I had always dreamt about. We talked about my retirement in another year and how we could plan annual escapes from the cold, dismal weather at home during February. We talked at length about our future plans, hopes for grandchildren, growing old together, and how happy we were at that moment in time. Maybe the local rum punch created this mythical perfect marriage scenario for me, but I believed it was real. Though we spent twenty-four hours together each day sharing our deepest thoughts and future dreams, I would later learn that even at this magical time, my husband had a very dark side and many secrets that he worked hard to keep from me.

This year, though, I couldn't escape the cold, long winter. I didn't have a traveling companion, couldn't afford to go anywhere, and remained overwhelmed by the responsibility my shoulders carried. But this year, I thanked God for making February a short month.

By the end of February, Sophia asked me about the plans I made to handle lambing. I told her, "I have no idea how this is going to work, but I have two weeks to get it figured out." We both prayed for guidance.

In the meantime, I still had eleven market lambs that needed to go to the butcher before the lambing barn could hold the new moms and babies. I asked Sophia if she knew anyone who had a truck or a way to transport the lambs twenty-five miles to the butcher. I called customers who previously expressed interest in buying a whole or half lamb and found enough people to fill all the orders. Some of the meat could also be sold in the store.

Sophia found someone who had a truck, and she brought it over to see if the truck panels left on the farm would fit the holes on the bed, but they did not. I called the butcher and got the name of a trucker willing to pick the lambs up and transport them. When I called the trucker, she was hesitant but said she could come between six and seven o'clock on the scheduled morning. The cost was more than I had wanted to spend, but I had to get the market lambs moved, and the meat and sheepskins would certainly generate some much-needed income.

The night before the truck arrived, I moved all the lambs into a pen near the door from which they would be loaded. Moving sheep isn't difficult if you get one to follow you. The rest typically follow wherever the leader goes. I grabbed some good hay, found a leader, and within a few minutes, the lambs settled into the pen for the night.

I didn't realize how connected the sheep are to their shepherd until the trucker came to load them up with me in the morning. She was prompt, professional, and used to hauling beef cattle. The lambs were scared and skittish. They each weighed between one hundred and one hundred fifty pounds, and it took a long time to get them to move onto the truck. The more we tried to coax them, the more they resisted. Finally, they were loaded and off to market. The experience stung me so much that I decided that day I wouldn't have strangers transport my animals anymore. I saw how easily they were loaded when they trusted the handler, and the shepherd was the best person to do the job. Fortunately, I had months to figure out how that would happen. But at that time, the very pregnant ewes had to be moved into the lambing barn, and preparations were made for the lambs that would soon arrive. I got the shepherd handbooks out of the bookcase and started studying.

CHAPTER 4

Lambing

The only thing I knew for sure about lambing that year was that the babies could arrive any time around March 7. Full shearing of the ewes and lambs took place on October 7, and the ewes moved in with Basil, the ram, shortly after that. Gestation for sheep takes about five months. I had no record of the order in which the ewes were bred except that all of them had been exposed at some point.

The pregnant ewes spent the winter in a large, open metal building with a cement lot and feed bunks for the hay. None of the buildings on the farm can be fully enclosed, some due to design and some because of disrepair. The only building that offered shelter from the elements had one open door and three interior pens with walls about four or five feet high. The walls protected the moms and babies from the wind, and wooden panels could be pieced together to create a four-square-foot individual pen, or jug, for each mom and her lambs. The lambing barn, as I called it, was nearest to the house and had electricity and lights in case I needed to check on an animal in the long, dark overnight hours. The size of the barn limited the number of ewes that could deliver on any single day. The moms stayed in the jugs for several days after lambing to ensure bonding and healthy starts for the lambs, and with enough individual jugs for maybe six or seven ewes, I waited for potential chaos to start.

Since the main shearing for the ewes took place in fall, when the animals came off pasture with cleaner fleeces, the next step after shipping off the market lambs was to arrange for a shearer to come and remove the wool from the bellies, udders, and backsides of the ewes to prepare for lambing. This partial shearing, called crutching, ideally happens before the babies arrive so they don't suck on wool when they try to nurse. Luckily, I called one of the shearers previously used, and he agreed to come that Saturday. He planned to fully shear Basil and Barney, since the rams and wethers stayed in full wool for breeding. Supposedly, the pheromones from their wool helps bring the ewes into heat. The shearer also agreed to trim the hooves of all the sheep for an extra dollar per animal.

On Friday night, I moved all the pregnant ewes, Basil, and Barney up to the lambing barn. Barney was a triplet and ended up being a bottle lamb when he was younger, so I usually counted on him to be my lead sheep. I brought a white grain bucket down by the sheep, which immediately got their attention. They only got grain in the morning, so the appearance of what looked like food in the afternoon became a curiosity. I called Barney, and he came right to me. I opened the gates, turned, and headed to the lambing barn. Barney took the lead, and all the rest of the sheep followed. Within five minutes, all the sheep had moved to their new home, and I was set for the shearer.

The shearer arrived early in the morning, and I helped him while Sophia watched the store. I bagged the wool from the boys and helped move the girls. Despite the bitter cold, everything went smoothly, and I felt tremendous relief upon task completion. I thought, *One step closer to lambing.*

While I waited for the lambs to arrive, I tried to get everything else in place. I looked through existing lambing supplies and listed the current inventory:

- green ear tags, but not enough if each ewe delivered at least one lamb
- several ear taggers
- Triodine, an iodine solution for the umbilical cords
- Nutri-Drench, a liquid nutrient-rich supplement for weak lambs
- small rubber bands for castrating males and docking tails
- banding tool for the rubber bands
- syringes in various sizes
- several unused 18G x ¾-inch needles
- SpectoGard to prevent E. coli in the new lambs
- feeding tube to fit the largest syringe
- penicillin in the refrigerator
- long, arm-length plastic gloves to help deliver stuck lambs
- black rubber lamb puller tool with adjustable loops on each end to put on lamb hooves to pull out stuck lambs that were partially delivered
- a small amount of lamb milk replacer

My previous experience with lambing primarily involved holding the baby lambs while my husband put the ear tags in, docked the tails, and castrated the males. The ewes rarely needed assistance delivering their lambs, but my husband did help with a couple sets of triplets. Before we got sheep on the farm, I attended an educational day at the University of Wisconsin-Madison sheep facility in Arlington and learned about their lambing practices. I used the information provided and my organizational skills to create lambing spreadsheets. I recorded the details for each ewe and her lambs—birth date, tag numbers, sex, birth weight, and a check-off for each required milestone. I printed blank spreadsheets each year and kept them with a pen and red clipboard to take out to the barn each day. I could then analyze the data and track the lambs' progress.

And I did have to pull a lamb once when my husband briefly left the farm and my favorite ewe, Mocha, couldn't deliver her first lamb, a fourteen-pound boy. Mocha's extreme distress prompted me to get instructions from my cell phone while in the barn. The process turned out to be pretty easy. The lamb's nose and front hooves had already appeared, so I just steadily pulled on the hooves, and the slippery lamb pretty much popped right out. Mocha was relieved, the baby was beautiful and healthy, and I almost passed out after it was over.

This year presented new challenges, as I was alone on the farm. I ordered more ear tags and some Pritchard nipples, a specific kind of nipple that worked well for bottle-feeding orphan lambs and was screwed right onto an empty soda bottle. Since I usually don't drink soda, as the one-eyed cleaning lady's husband could attest, I asked my knitting friends if they could save any empty soda bottles from their homes and donate to the cause. To my surprise, they not only brought in bags of empty bottles, but several of them also volunteered to help with the lambs. I programmed their phone numbers into my cell phone as well as that of my veterinarian and felt a little more prepared.

I knew that as the ewes got closer to delivery day, their udders would swell to the point that they looked like they would burst. So I tried to be proactive and moved a few of the ewes with very large udders into the most sheltered pen. On March 5, I walked into the barn to find that my oldest ewe, Brownie, delivered her lambs overnight. A big, healthy male lamb nursed vigorously, while a cold, lifeless female lamb lay next to Brownie, her afterbirth puddled in the corner of the pen. Not all of the sheep receive names—only the special ones and the really naughty ones. Brownie gained notoriety for a little bit of each.

Brownie came to the farm years earlier as part of the original twenty ewes and one ram. We wanted livestock primarily to produce manure for organic farming and gardening. I walked into a yarn store to get some materials one day, and the owner asked if I knew anyone who wanted to buy some Romney sheep. She planned to start a new breed and needed a home for her existing ewes. I called my husband and asked if we could a get a few. He offered to buy all twenty. When we brought the sheep home, we noticed that we only had nineteen, but had to go back to pick up the ram. We offered to settle for nineteen ewes and a ram, but the owner insisted we take another ewe, which turned out to be a beautiful little lamb with brown fiber that looked like dreadlocks. We named her Brownie. Younger and smaller than the rest, we felt sorry for how she had to fight for food. When shearing came and we felt her fiber, we knew she had the most luxurious wool on the entire farm. She still does. When an international knitwear designer came from Sweden and visited the farm, she bought some yarn made from Brownie's fiber to take back home.

The problem with Brownie was that she had always been a horrible mother. The first year she had twins, she tried to leap the walls to get away from them. The next year, we had to pin her against the barn wall to let the babies nurse. Each year, we fed her lambs by bottle because she refused to take care of them. The third year, she had twins again. She took care of one lamb and rejected the other. I wanted to cull her, but my husband insisted we keep her, if only for her amazing fiber. The fourth year, she had twin girls and took care of both of them beautifully. We thought the streak had ended. But seeing the dead lamb in her pen made me doubt her maturity and mothering abilities. I didn't know if Brownie's lamb was stillborn or died from neglect, but the answer wasn't going to bring her back to life. I got the pitchfork and sadly removed the afterbirth and dead lamb, carrying them along with the bedding underneath them to the burial spot behind one of the farthest buildings.

I then built a jug for Brownie and her lamb with some wooden panels, filled a five-gallon bucket with fresh water, and gave her some hay. I dipped the lamb's umbilical cord in the iodine solution and then let them bond for the rest of the day, knowing that the next day, I needed to find the courage to do the lambing tasks that I had previously only observed. I texted my five lambing volunteers, announcing the first birth and soliciting help to hold the lamb for me at nine o'clock the next morning. The first response came from Jocelyn, Jo for short.

Jo took beginning knitting lessons from me and became a good knitter very quickly. She was preparing for her wedding later in the year, and her brother, Alan, had just moved from Florida to be closer to family and help with the wedding. They both were homeschooled in North Carolina and felt very comfortable around livestock. She was very excited to be the first volunteer selected for lambing duties. Overnight, I decided that I wasn't going to castrate Brownie's lamb. I justified my fear because it was her first male lamb and he was absolutely gorgeous. But I still had the other tasks.

Brownie took great care of her first male lamb.

When Jo arrived, we weighed the lamb and recorded his weight—sixteen pounds. I gave him two squirts of SpectoGard, loaded one rubber band on the band holder, and carefully slid it up his tail. When it got to the point that I could see the skin folds, I released the band onto the tail. He didn't even flinch—docking done. The rubber band cuts off the circulation and the tail falls off within a few weeks. This method certainly proved easier and more humane than some of the other methods. I loaded up the ear tagger with green tag number one, but when I tried to tag the ear, I didn't have the strength to pierce it. *Surely, the tagger must be defective,* I thought.

Later that day, I talked with my supplier, who previously had interned at University of Wisconsin-Madison's sheep facility and had her own flock of sheep. She offered to bring an orthopedic tagger when she dropped off the ear tags that I had ordered. I had an orthopedic stapler at the office but never thought to inquire about assisted ear taggers. She stopped after the store closed and said the tagger had to be special ordered and wouldn't arrive for a few weeks but offered to look at the defective tagger. We went into the lambing barn, she tried the tagger on the lamb, and it worked just fine. She suggested I use both hands to squeeze it together and offered tips on the exact positioning of the ear tag, between the two cartilage ridges in the ear. That was exactly the training that I needed. The ear tags would later go in quite easily, once I knew what I was doing.

Concerned that I would miss another birth gone wrong, I started checking the ewes more frequently. I checked on them at eleven o'clock before I went to bed and as soon as I woke up in the morning, sometimes as early as five thirty. With feeding the animals, working in the store seven days a week, and not getting enough sleep, I walked around exhausted most days. I continued to pray for help, and God kept sending me willing volunteers. Jo's brother, Alan, came over to help several times a week. He loved the animals and loved to help. He offered to carry water buckets and pitch hay for me. He held the lambs more than any of the other volunteers.

The next few ewes delivered healthy female lambs until March 10, when Scrapie tag number fifty delivered twins, one boy and one girl. I read up on castration and successfully banded the male. It worked similarly to tail docking, but I really wanted to be sure that nothing went wrong. Lambing was well underway.

Alan helped me set up the creep area once the ewes and their lambs left the jugs and moved back to the large metal building. He put some panels together to create a separate area with wooden slats that the lambs could fit through but the mothers couldn't. The lambs had extra protection and access to the best hay and could rejoin their mothers for nursing whenever they wanted. Within a few days, the lambs started playing with each other, running, and jumping. They brought much joy to the most dismal days.

Lambing progressed smoothly for the first two weeks, but then ten lambs were born within twenty-four hours, including the first set of triplets. Sheep udders have two nipples, and my ewes could handle twins easily. But triplets presented problems. First of all, triplet babies typically weigh less than the average ten to twelve pounds. Second, the smallest lamb never seems to get enough milk, struggles, and eventually dies. I asked a lot of shepherds how they handle triplets, but the best answer came from the sheep facility at University of Wisconsin-Madison. The shepherd there tried grafting—trying to force a ewe with a single to take one of the triplets—without much success because most ewes only feed their own lambs by their scent. So he suggested pulling the largest lamb, which will eagerly take a bottle, and letting the smallest lamb, which needs the most help, to nurse with mom.

Knowing this, I let the triplets nurse for the first twenty-four to forty-eight hours to get the vital colostrum and then pulled the largest triplet and started feeding lamb milk replacer from a recycled soda bottle with the Pritchard nipple. It worked beautifully. Now my list of tasks included feeding a baby lamb five times daily until it could drink enough at one feeding to lengthen the time between feedings. I made a sign for the front door of the store that read, "Checking lambs—back in ten minutes." Nobody complained about the wait. Alan frequently volunteered to help with bottle feeding, even though it took longer for him to drive to the farm than it would take to feed the lamb.

The bigger problem came when three more lambs arrived in the next two days. I didn't have the room for each mom to have a jug. I made makeshift pens in the larger open areas with panels that Jo and Alan built from scrap wood on the farm. I ran out of water pails and had to improvise with old feeding troughs. The barn echoed with crying lambs and ewes trying to discern whose baby needed to be fed. The overcrowding wasn't conducive to bonding, but it was the best I could offer. Some of the lambs escaped the makeshift pens, and I needed to cross-reference my spreadsheets to know from which pen the lamb came. I prayed for a break in the lamb arrivals, but three more came the next day and another three the following day. Each lamb looked more beautiful than the last. I loved to climb into the pens and hold them, snuggling into their soft, woolly bodies, until their mother started bellowing and stomping her feet. Then I climbed into the next pen and held more lambs. I'm sure that God created baby lambs to be so incredibly adorable that they would bring immeasurable joy to me at this point in my life.

All the lambs looked good except for one smaller set of twins. The male lamb weighed only 7.25 pounds at birth, while his sister weighed in at 9.5 pounds. The little guy always seemed to be crying for milk and not connecting with his mom for whatever reason. On the second day, I came into the barn to find him motionless in the jug. He was alive but incredibly weak. I put my finger in his mouth, and he was cold. If I did nothing, he certainly would die. The barn was cold, and he was too weak to suck, even though his mother was trying very hard to take care of him. I knew he wouldn't make it through the night, so I tucked him inside my winter coat and carried him into the house. I had a neck wrap filled with flax seed that I put in the microwave for two minutes; I covered it in a bath towel and wrapped it around his little body. I grabbed the Nutri-Drench and gave him a squirt, but there was no response.

My only other option was to get the feeding tube and try to put some milk directly into his stomach. I prayed that God would help me to not kill him in the process, but I knew that if I didn't try this last resort, I would end up killing him by not helping. Fearless, I mixed up some warm lamb milk replacer, filled the largest syringe, and attached the sterile feeding tube. I straightened his neck, inserted the feeding tube, which went in quite easily, and filled his tummy with warm milk. Within twenty minutes, he was standing and crying. I cried for joy. "Thank You, God!" I exclaimed. I kept him in the house overnight, feeding him with a bottle a few times until he could suck vigorously. The next morning, I reunited him with his mother, and he started nursing right away. He grew up to be a fine, healthy lamb.

I figured out quickly that the older and more experienced ewes bred first. Toward the end of March and early April, the yearlings started delivering singles. Some of them knew what to do, and others required patience. But the earlier crowd of babies had moved into the larger building, and I appreciated the extra space for the first-time moms. I continued to check on them several times a day just in case one of them needed help.

One afternoon in early April, I heard a horrible sound coming from the lambing barn. It sounded like a sheep got caught in something and made a horrible moaning, screaming sound. I put the sign up on the front of the store, locked the door, and quickly went to check on the commotion. I found a yearling standing and straining with her lamb hanging halfway out. The lamb was large, wet, and very stuck. Instead of the normal presentation of two hooves and the nose, only one leg, the entire head, and part of the shoulders appeared. This definitely looked abnormal, so I immediately called the vet. The nice lady who answered the phone detected my sheer panic but calmly explained that all the veterinarians were out on call and when one became available, it would take at least twenty minutes to get to the farm. I tried pulling the lamb, but the ewe just screamed louder and fell to the ground. I told the nice lady at the vet clinic, "I'm sure the lamb is dead, but I just don't want to lose the mom too." She encouraged me to be patient, and she would send someone as soon as possible. I hung up the phone, and my heart was racing. Desperate to help the ewe, I ran to the house and grabbed one of the shepherd books.

Sure enough, the book contained an entire section on lambing problems, including the one I faced. I prayed that God would help me follow the brief instructions specifically as written. I ran back to the barn and laid the ewe down on the floor so that the lamb was positioned with its stuck leg toward the ceiling. I then turned and pulled the lamb in a corkscrew manner, just like the book instructed, and it came unstuck. As soon as the lamb was born, the ewe turned and started licking it, just like an experienced mom. Instinct kicked in for her, and she started caring for her lamb. I cried, relieved that the ewe survived, but also because she would soon discover her baby was dead. To my surprise, the baby lamb started moving, breathing, and eventually crying. I couldn't believe the miracle that had just taken place. I picked up my cell phone to cancel the vet call and noticed that the time I hung up from their office was just five minutes earlier. I don't know how that was even possible, but I'm sure God's hand helped me in that barn.

I called the vet clinic and explained what happened, and the receptionist cheered me on. She sounded just as surprised and excited as I was. I then got a syringe and a sterile needle and gave the ewe a shot of penicillin to prevent any infection from the trauma. Within a few minutes, the baby lamb started nursing successfully, and I returned to the store. The waiting customers were amazed by the story. I could hardly believe what just happened, except that I experienced it firsthand.

Why would I experience all of these troubles with lambing when nothing like this had happened in the previous years? And why would God create this miracle for me? This miracle wasn't something I felt responsible for creating. God used me as a tool to help these beautiful creatures. And He needed to teach me something about His love for me. God can do the impossible. Sometimes we need to learn to trust God to help us in impossible situations. Then we can see His miracles.

CHAPTER 5

Spring Arrives

Before all fifty-one lambs arrived, the farm cats started having their kittens. I heard some of them in the lambing barn one day and peered over one of the walls to see a litter of five kittens, each one unique. I recognized the mother cat when she came to take care of them, and she didn't mind when I reached in with a gloved hand to lift each kitten up for a closer peek. She picked a great spot for them inside a space about six inches wide between the barn walls. They would be safe there until they grew enough to escape, and I could enjoy them each day when I came to feed the bottle lambs.

Farm cats became a necessity on the farm, as on most farms, to control the rodent population. Since I live near a bird refuge and enjoy the great variety of birds that surround the farm and come to rest on my land, I don't believe in using poisons or chemicals. The original four farm cats came as kittens from my aunt's farm, and she was happy to part with them. New tom cats come around often from neighboring farms, and I now have cats of just about every color—orange, black, white, gray, calico, tabbies, and even a purebred Siamese. Dolce, the Siamese cat, actually came as an adult but has lived on the farm for almost eight years. She doesn't like any of the other cats, and she doesn't like any people except for me. I allowed her to live in the house basement one very cold winter, and she has been grateful ever since.

Once the kittens started arriving, I found them all over the farm. Some lived in the hay barn, some in empty bushel baskets in the workshop, and the cat named Prolific Breeder decided to keep her litter in the middle of the lamb's creep pen. Most of the cats don't have names except to identify some particular characteristic. Dolce came to the farm with a name and got to keep it. I only know of one litter that Dolce produced, and Prolific Breeder, who got her name because she produces more kittens than any other cat on the farm, is the only surviving cat from that litter. Prolific Breeder turned out to be a very friendly cat despite her mother's quirkiness. She is a great mouser, takes her kittens hunting, and thrives on human contact.

I'm not sure why Prolific Breeder chose the creep pen to raise her family, but the kittens grew up with the lambs and started acting like them. They climbed up on the backs of the sheep and snuggled in their wool to nap. When I came to deliver hay, they got excited and climbed in and around the hay piles while the lambs nibbled away. When it came time for the lambs to go out to pasture each day, the lamby kitties followed them out and came back when they returned to the barn. Wherever the lambs went, the kittens followed.

A lamby kitty snuggles into the warm wool of an accommodating lamb.

As the kittens in the barn wall grew, their mother moved them behind a large square bale of hay in one of the sheds. Shortly after the move, I noticed the kittens walking around crying, obviously looking for their mother. I couldn't find her anywhere. I didn't have much time to look for her, since I needed to get to the bank and post office before I opened the store. But on my way into town, I caught a glimpse of her. Unfortunately, she had wandered into the highway and was hit by a car. When I returned from my errands, I grabbed a shovel, removed her dead body from the road, and gave her a proper burial. Now the dilemma became what to do with her five kittens.

I never had a mother cat expire before her kittens grew up, but I thought it might be worth a shot to see if Prolific Breeder would help raise them. That evening, I gathered the five kittens in an old bath towel and carried them down to the lamb's creep pen. Fortunately, Prolific Breeder was there nursing her lamby kitties. I petted her while the kittens nursed and then gradually snuck in the extra five kittens. I don't think Prolific Breeder or any of the lamby kitties even noticed. The orphaned kittens were so hungry that they latched right on to get some good food. When I checked on them the next morning, I counted all ten kittens. Over time, the five orphaned kittens moved out of the creep pen and back with the other farm cats. But the lamby kitties continued to live with the sheep.

Eventually, the snow melted, and spring officially arrived. Easter fell later in April, and I looked forward to a long weekend. But before I could enjoy three days off from the store and the arrival of my children for a long Easter celebration, I had pressing farm issues that needed tending.

A year earlier, my husband and I owned three farms. Two of them sold, and I lived on 155 acres with the house and the outbuildings as well as all the livestock and the retail store. My husband was the fifth generation of his family to live on this farm, and many of his relatives didn't want me to stay. Because of the abrupt change in my life, I put it all in God's hands. I prepared to be evicted from my home, and I prayed that God would clearly, unequivocally show me His plan.

I never planned to be a farmer. As a child, as a college student, and throughout my adult career, I never once said, "My dream is to be a farmer." Since I was a foreign exchange student to Bangkok when I was sixteen and traveled extensively throughout my adult career, I thought maybe this was the time for God to use me in international mission work. I even downloaded an application for an assistant position with a mission office in Prague and scheduled an appointment with my pastors. But I wasn't sure that this was God's calling at that particular time. I needed to wait on God and hear His plan for my life. So I continued to pray for direction and to clearly hear what God wanted me to do.

Sophia prayed for guidance and answers. She knew that one of the risks for her was that the store could close at any time. She also prayed for healing for everyone involved. My Bible study ladies and prayer partners prayed for direction for my life. I knew that God would answer in His time, but the waiting was painful. And until I got an answer, I had to keep managing the farm. I knew that crops had to be planted within a few weeks, and I knew that I couldn't possibly take on that responsibility myself, so I started searching for land renters.

I pulled out the crop reporting maps and determined how much land was allocated for hay and pasture and how much land could potentially be rented. I talked with other landowners to find out current rental rates for farmland. Other farmers in the area received $135–200 per acre. I started calling some of the renters and asked if they might be interested in renting more land. Some of them seemed interested but couldn't commit to another seventy-one acres.

One night, after attending a Wednesday midweek Lenten service, I stopped at the grocery store to pick up a few items. As soon as I walked in, I recognized Bart, a friend of mine from Rotary. As we got caught up on events, I mentioned how busy the farm kept me and that the newest dilemma looming in front of me involved finding potential land renters. Bart just happened to be a lending officer in the agricultural division of the local bank and knew several farmers who were looking to rent land. He asked if he could give them my contact information, and I quickly wrote down my e-mail address and phone numbers. He made no promises but offered to help in any way he could.

Because of the complexity of my situation, the decision of whether I could stay in my home on the farm or would be forced to leave had to go through the courts. I hired an attorney to represent me and prepared for the court hearing scheduled for the morning of April 15. My attorney asked me to arrive early to go over some papers she prepared for the hearing. When I got there, her assistant greeted me at the courthouse entrance and ushered me into one of the meeting rooms. As soon as we sat down, the paralegal informed me that my attorney was at another court hearing in another county and wouldn't be arriving for my hearing on time—and possibly not at all. The best she could offer was that my attorney would try to call in by telephone if she got a chance.

Shocked and stunned, I asked if we could reschedule the hearing. Because the land decisions were so time-sensitive, that was not an option. The paralegal told me she could sit next to me in the courtroom but could not represent me. I had to do the best I could on my own. My immediate thought was that I might be heading to Prague after all. But I started praying that God would give me the right words to say at the right time and to help me not get flustered. I also prayed that, by some miracle, my attorney would show up and represent me.

As we walked into the courtroom, I felt completely out of place. The paralegal sat beside me, smiled warmly, and said, "Just answer the questions the best you can." As I sat there and listened to the proceedings, I wanted to scream at what I heard. Clearly, a group of people wanted me off the farm, even though I was never part of the decisions that put me in the situation I was in. But I sat still and speechless until the questions were directed toward me.

Finally, I was asked to state my position. As soon as I started speaking, the court reporter interrupted. My attorney had just dialed in by phone. I was then asked if it was all right for the attorney to represent me. Without hesitation, I let her take over. She was prepared, and though not physically present, she stated a clear case for allowing me to stay on the farm for the time being. At the end of the hearing, the court ordered that I could stay on the farm as long as I could provide a fully executed rental agreement for at least $250 an acre within ten days. My heart sank at such a monumental task, since I didn't know anybody who rented their land for such a high price.

When I got back to the store, I told Sophia what happened. She offered to continue praying, and we both knew that I would accept whatever God planned for me. I called a local attorney who handled farm leases and scheduled to meet with him the next morning to draw up a lease, just in case I could find a renter within the week. That afternoon, in between waiting on yarn customers, I fielded angry calls from my husband's relatives screaming at me about how I didn't belong there. When they called the store phone, I politely said, "I'm sorry, I'm helping other customers right now," and I hung up. Then my cell phone started ringing. I didn't answer it and didn't look forward to going through the angry voice mails and texts. I was beginning to feel like leaving the farm would be the best for me so I could get away from all the evil that my husband brought into my life. But it wasn't my decision after all. God got to decide.

At about four thirty that afternoon, before I closed the store, I checked my e-mail one last time. I saw an e-mail address in my inbox that I didn't recognize. I opened the e-mail, and the message was brief. The dairy farmer asked if my farmland was still available to rent. He received my contact information from his banker, Bart, and was willing to pay $275 per acre for rent. I picked up the phone, called Sophia, and exclaimed, "Our prayers are answered!"

CHAPTER 6

New Life, New Hope

Easter celebrates new life in Christ through His death and resurrection. This message of hope brings joy to me and my family each year. But this year, the celebration was even more glorious. I saw how Jesus triumphed over Satan and evil and how His triumphant battles brought new life for me and all believers. And I also saw how Jesus walked alongside me, guiding and encouraging me. Jesus is alive indeed! And He lives in me and through me.

My children came home to celebrate Easter with me. After church, we spent much of the day outside, soaking up the sunshine and watching lots of baby lambs frolicking. Everybody held a few lambs, found some eggs for the annual Easter egg hunt, and enjoyed abundant food and family time together. As much joy and happiness as I feel whenever my kids come home, I always feel sad when they leave. This feeling doesn't last long, because I know they are grown and have lives of their own, but I love them very much and miss them when our time together ends.

The day after Easter, life on the farm got back to the normal daily routine of feeding and caring for the animals, working in the store, and planning for gardens and pastures. This year, the workload would be much heavier, because once the snow completely melted, I saw the mess on my hands. In previous years, I took care of the house, helped out in the store, and went into the buildings designated for the sheep, llamas, and alpacas. I never really looked in the rest of the buildings or took responsibility for what happened in them. That was my husband's domain.

Opening the doors to some of the buildings revealed huge piles of junk and garbage. Each building contained dozens of containers of waste oil sitting in five-gallon pails, open buckets, and pans. I don't think any oil had left the farm in the previous ten years. Partially empty containers of agricultural chemicals, pesticides, herbicides, and coated seed were left behind. Outside the buildings, I discovered five piles of junk with old wood, metal, bicycles, truck parts, dehumidifiers, and roofing materials. I found hundreds of nuts and bolts underneath large hay bales. Jim came home to help one weekend and started sorting and organizing. He found three weed eaters and five chain saws, but none of them worked. One of the buildings still housed all the horse-drawn farm equipment that hadn't been used since the 1940s.

I took pictures and got estimates to hire someone to remove everything that had no future use on the farm. Even with getting a dumpster and getting volunteers to fill it, the disposal costs still came to more than $6,000. I just couldn't afford it at that time or for a long time. When my neighbor learned of the mess on the farm, she talked with her husband about helping out. He came the next day to assess the situation, and within a week, he and his wife had emptied all the waste oil and hauled it away. They sorted and organized multiple containers of unopened oil that will last me a lifetime. They also took some of the garbage that was too big for me to haul to the dump and returned with a fifty-five-gallon burn barrel for me to start burning some of the other waste safely. With their help to start cleaning up some of the buildings, my spirits lifted, even though the farm still had a lot more garbage to deal with.

Trying to balance the costs of cleanup, the cost of operating the farm, and the volume of physical work that needed to be done each day overwhelmed me. In fact, I wasn't sure how long I could afford to stay on the farm long-term. I would have to refinance the farm if I was going to keep it by myself, and I wasn't really sure how that would be possible.

A group of ladies came to knit each Thursday night at the yarn shop. Some of them arranged their work schedules around this weekly social time. Many of the women moved to the area from other states and made new friends at the yarn shop with other fiber artists who shared their interests. On any given Thursday night, somebody might be knitting, spinning, or crocheting. More experienced artisans helped the newbies. The group called themselves the Ewesful Fiber Club, and they turned out to be quite resourceful.

As hard as I tried to keep my personal life private, I lived in a small rural community, and my husband's difficulties quickly became the talk of the town. People were shocked, and some of the ladies stayed late on knit night to talk privately with me about the rumors they heard. They couldn't believe what was being said and wanted me to know what was going on. I already knew some of the truth and confirmed parts of the stories that were true. They were shocked yet incredibly sympathetic and supportive. They all knew that I had just retired from a lucrative position a few months earlier and wondered aloud at how I would possibly manage on my own. I wondered the same thing, especially when I heard that some people were boycotting the store because of what my husband had done. In addition to the intense humiliation I suffered because of my husband, I was being shunned and hurt financially because of his actions.

One night, the knitting ladies started an open discussion about my future on the farm. They went through all the options they could think of, including returning to my former position. When I explained that the time limit to reinstate all my securities and insurance licenses had passed and I would basically have to start over, they agreed that wasn't a good choice. When they asked how I could possibly afford to stay on the farm, I quietly explained that I had no idea but needed to trust God. They suggested looking into low-interest loan programs for women and gave me sources to seek out. But then they also decided to initiate some fundraisers to help generate money for me to stay on the farm.

I didn't know most of these women very well, but I was touched by their compassion and enthusiasm. One of them had a degree in art and offered to design a T-shirt. One of them suggested creating a calendar with farm pictures to sell in the store. And some of them slipped me twenty-dollar bills when nobody else was looking.

Later in the week, some of the ladies returned to the store with other family members to share very personal stories about similar ordeals they endured and offered their love and support. When I was having a difficult day, God always seemed to send in one of these ladies with a smile, cup of coffee, or knitting project to sit down and visit a while. Their kindness and generosity helped me survive and showed me that whenever light shines on the darkness, much goodness is revealed.

I needed a lot of light during those very dark days. In addition to the mess in and around the outbuildings, the pasture fencing was disastrous. Some of the fencing was electric, and some pastures had wire netting; some had a combination of each. As the grass started growing, I anxiously wanted to get the sheep out to pasture, but I wasn't prepared for that to happen in so many ways. One day, the llamas and alpacas decided to break through a weak fence and let themselves out. A passerby on the highway saw them and stopped in, offering to help. I couldn't leave the store, so I agreed to let him help. None of the animals had been vaccinated yet for Clostridium Perfringens Types C & D and Clostridium Tetanus Toxoid (CD/T), so I was concerned that they would bloat if left out all day. Within twenty minutes, he returned to report they were all contained. I still have no idea how he did it, but I was grateful for his quick thinking.

When I looked at the fencing, I saw that most of it couldn't hold any animals in. Wires were down, netting wasn't high enough to prevent an agile sheep from jumping over it, and I had to make decisions. With plenty of hay to still feed, I decided to find a section that looked secure and start introducing the sheep to the pasture in short periods of time. I started with twenty minutes one day and then an hour the next. By the end of two weeks, they could safely be out on pasture for most of the day, but I still only had a small area secure enough to hold them. I didn't have time to fix most of the fencing, because I also had a garden that needed planting.

Earlier in spring, when I looked for additional sources of income for the farm, I decided to offer community-supported agriculture (CSA) shares. CSA involves selling shares upfront to customers who would then receive weekly bags of fresh organic produce for twenty weeks throughout the summer. Alan volunteered to rototill my garden that had been fertilized with sheep manure the previous fall. Jo agreed to do a volunteer CSA share for which she would come each week to help plant, weed, and harvest in exchange for fresh produce. I already had ten families that paid the fee to be part of this venture. Seeds and organic bedding plants needed to get in the ground to start growing.

Fortunately, I love to garden, and this diversion always fills me with hope. To push a seed into the ground, put a little water on it, and watch it sprout and grow never ceases to amaze me. The seeds I used each year germinated very well and grew to be strong, healthy plants. I drew up a map of where to put the different varieties, and the seeds got planted. By Memorial Day, everything was on schedule for produce deliveries to start in a few weeks.

Organic seeds grow quickly into plants for the garden.

With the garden started, I turned my attention back to the pastures. Actually, I couldn't avoid the issue, because something always needed repair. One sunny day, Jim's girlfriend, Kristina, offered to help in the store so I could get some more outdoor work finished. A volunteer farmer stopped by to offer his help with making hay. As we stood there discussing baling equipment on the farm, he noticed a little white lamb alone at the far end of the one pasture. That certainly was unusual, because the lambs typically stuck close to their mothers and the rest of the flock. After he left, I walked down to see what was wrong. I didn't know that miles of old electrical wiring laid buried in the pasture grass, and the poor lamb was entangled and in serious trouble. I tried to free her, but somehow, in her panicked state, she had wrapped the wire tightly around several of her legs, neck, and abdomen. The wool was caught so tightly that I couldn't even see how much wire threatened her life. Each time that I got one loop unwrapped from her leg, I realized it was pulling on her neck or another leg. I ran back to the shed and started looking for a wire cutter, but it was like looking for a needle in a haystack under piles of tools and junk. I didn't even know where to begin.

Then I remembered that I had a pair of pliers down in the store that could cut wire, so I ran down to retrieve it. When Kristina saw me rush in, she knew immediately that something was wrong. As I explained the situation, one of the Ewesful Fiber Club ladies who had stopped in to knit jumped up and volunteered to come help me. Kaylee wore a lovely blouse and nice pair of slacks that day. I explained that the pasture had lots of dirt and manure, and the lamb was quite distressed. She insisted on coming to help. Kaylee explained that she was a registered nurse, loved animals, and had previously worked in a vet clinic. I told her to follow me, and we raced down the pasture lane to the struggling white lamb.

I'm sure that God brought Kaylee into the store that day for a very particular reason. I desperately needed her help and skills. As she carefully held the lamb, I cut away the tangled mess of wire. Soon all the lamby kitties arrived to help, climbing on the lamb and Kaylee's leg, brushing against me as I continued cutting the wire off the lamb. Despite the dire situation, I couldn't help but smile. The sun shone brightly, the lamb had no injuries, and Kaylee brought much calm and peace to me that day.

As soon as the lamb was free, it scampered off to the barn, followed closely by the lamby kitties. Kaylee stayed and asked how I was doing. I explained the situation, and she offered to stay and pull up the remaining wire buried in the grass. She didn't care how dirty she would get or how messy the job would be; she genuinely cared and wanted to help in any way she could. As we pulled up wire, she asked if I needed any additional help. I told her how behind I was on vaccinating the animals, and she scheduled a time to come back and help vaccinate. Jo and a few other volunteers came to help too, and all the animals got vaccinated within a few hours.

Touched by the compassion of others, I am reminded of God's immense love for His children. He knows our every need and the troubles we will face even before we know them. Time and again, He puts human angels in our lives to help get us through difficult situations. How is it that the exact people with the specific skills that I needed just happened to be there? God amazed me with his careful timing, and it didn't happen just once.

The Ewesful Fiber Club continued meeting on Thursday nights, but as summer vacations started, the usual dozen or so ladies dwindled to a handful. Each person brought such a unique perspective that the conversations remained lively. I opened all the store windows one balmy night as we knit and chatted. All of a sudden, the alpacas and llamas in the nearest building started humming and calling. We looked out the window to see them all standing in a line along the fence, facing east. Something had their attention, and we joined their curiosity. As we headed to the front door, I saw exactly why they seemed alarmed. Twenty-three ewes headed single file across the hay field and toward the highway.

I asked the ladies to watch the store while I tried to get them redirected. But there was no way they wanted to be left out of the excitement. They dropped their knitting and followed me out of the store. All of us that night were well over fifty years of age, and many spent more time knitting in a chair than running on a treadmill. But they were ready for anything. As I ran across the driveway to head off the sheep before they reached the highway, one of the ladies scaled the pasture fence and started running and screaming, "What should I do? Tell me how to help!"

I asked her to stand at the corner and make sure nobody moved beyond her while I went to get a grain bucket. By the time I got back, everyone else had joined her, anxious for an assignment. I asked some of them to stay in specific locations to block escape routes and some of them to open gates for me. One of the ladies asked why so many cats were out with the sheep, and I simply explained that the lamby kitties always showed up to help with the sheep.

Once the pasture fence was opened up, I found ewe number thirteen to be my leader sheep. She was always easy to spot, since her tail was longer than all the rest. I banged on the side of the grain bucket to get her attention, and she came running toward me. The rest followed her, and we started a long, winding parade back to the barn. The knitting ladies kept their positions, closed gates as we passed through, and returned to the store to marvel at the adventures they never expected to have at knitting night. One of the ladies was disappointed that it didn't take very long to get them all back in. I think she had visions of roping and dragging each individual animal instead of using their natural behavior to get them to go back where they were supposed to be. I'm sure when the ladies returned home to their families, they enjoyed sharing their adventures. Some still talk about what a crazy night it was.

With the sheep secured for the night, I woke early the next day to find out how they escaped. I wasn't sure where they got out, but I got some temporary fence posts and shored up areas where the wire netting looked low. Still, it didn't seem plausible that all twenty-three ewes would have jumped a fence at the exact same spot. Since they paraded along the east side of the pasture, I naturally assumed they had crossed the entire pasture and exited on the east side before heading south to the road. Boy, was I wrong.

The next day, the sheep went out to pasture and came back several times like usual. Typically, they went out at daybreak, ate for a while, and then came back to the barn to get water and chew their cud in the shade. They made the trip out to pasture and back to rest several times throughout the day. After the store closed, I could see them grazing peacefully out in the pasture and thought all was good. I followed my normal routine, made my supper, and ate it in the dining room. I read the paper, and when I came back into the kitchen with my dirty supper dishes, I looked out the window to see the same twenty-three ewes grazing on the lawn right outside the back door. The sun was setting, and I could barely see them in the dusk. I quickly rushed outside and opened the gate down by the barn. But instead of going where they should be for the night, they scattered. Some ran behind the outbuildings, tromping over the piles of debris; some ran back toward the pasture, and some just kept grazing, enjoying the special treat of sweet grass.

I knew I could never get the sheep back in by myself in the dark. So I called Alan. He was just fifteen minutes away, and I hoped he was home. To my surprise, he said, "We'll be there in one, maybe two minutes." What? He explained that he, Jo, and her fiancé were heading back from a day trip to New Glarus and had just driven past the farm. They were less than a mile away. As soon as they could turn around, they would be back. "Thank You, God," I said out loud.

Within five minutes, the sheep were penned and secure. The next day, I drove around the entire perimeter of the pasture and was shocked to find a ten-foot section of fencing opened up wide enough to drive a truck through into the hay field. Of course, the sheep walked right through. But this fence breach was at the farthest northwest spot in the pasture, a place that I would never have thought to look. It looked like the wires had been cut and a section of fence pulled wide open.

I am so incredibly thankful that God intervened to thwart some wicked, evil plan. To get to the east side of the farm near the store, where the escaped ewes first were spotted, meant that the sheep had to walk more than a half-mile around the entire perimeter of the outermost pasture fencing. If the sheep had headed south right away instead of north, they would have gotten lost in the corn fields or marsh. They showed up lost at the location where I happened to be with help available to get them back where they belonged. The second night, I could see the trampled grass where they walked along the outside of the fencing all the way up to the yard. Once again, the lost sheep appeared exactly where I was located to see them and within minutes of help to get them back in.

I often think about the song that declares how great God's faithfulness is to us. That's exactly how God chooses to work in our lives. When we are surrounded by darkness and evil and look to Him for guidance, comfort, and help, He responds with an amazing light to shine on and in us. Sometimes His light shows us things we don't want to see, but the darkness can never withstand the light. God's amazing light always fills us with new life and new hope.

CHAPTER 7

The Garden

It all began in a garden. Genesis records the account of Adam and Eve in the garden of Eden. The garden provided everything they needed; yet they wanted more. They wanted what they thought they needed instead of trusting God to provide everything their hearts desired. Much of what happened on the farm started with the garden. The sheep first arrived on the farm because they provided much-needed fertilizer for organic gardening. And the first clue that something seriously was wrong with my marriage happened in the garden.

Organic gardening involves creating a miniature ecosystem of plants, soil nutrients, and beneficial insects. I first learned about organic gardening by attending conferences and workshops and putting the ideas learned there into practice. Much can be learned firsthand through trial and error and gaining knowledge through experiences. With Alan and Jo's help, the garden had a great start. The garden location lay almost in the middle of the 155-acre farm on slightly sloping land. In years of drought, the lower land required far less watering than the higher ground. In wet years, the higher ground ensured that not all of the crops would be washed out or drowned. The entire perimeter of the garden was enclosed with netted fencing. Sometimes I used chicken wire, and sometimes I used extra wire netting from the sheep pastures. A large twelve-foot swinging wire gate opened for easy access with the garden tractor and little cart that I used to haul water into the garden and fresh produce out.

The fencing primarily kept animals out, not just wayward sheep, but white-tailed deer, coyotes, raccoons, and skunks that lived nearby. Animals that fit through the wire fence usually found their way into one of the live traps I set throughout the garden. Over time, I caught fewer and fewer rodents as the farm cats wandered farther into the adjacent hay fields to hunt and as I reduced the overall rodent population. The first year of organic gardening, I caught thirty-three chipmunks and ground squirrels, all of which were carried live up to the farm cats and released. The cats got great practice hunting and enhanced their supplemental cat food diet, and I always thought it was fair enough to the rodent to be able to escape in the open area.

Without the use of prohibited chemicals, pesticides, and herbicides, the selection and placement of plants in an organic garden is somewhat strategic. I started having much greater success when I utilized specific herbs and flowers. Calendula, marigolds, and nasturtium attract beneficial insects, such as honeybees and predatory wasps, while pungent herbs like rosemary, thyme, dill, cilantro, and mint not only keep the bad bugs at bay, but also enhance the flavor of compatible vegetables planted nearby. I'm convinced that parsley and marjoram help my tomatoes. Since I started utilizing companion planting, insects and other common garden pests rarely appear.

I don't always have success with every vegetable every year. I haven't figured out why some years, I have a bumper crop of cucurbits, and other years, I harvest very few zucchinis and am overwhelmed with potatoes. But I'm always learning and trying to improve.

By midsummer, most of the vegetables were producing well. CSA members commented on the delicious varieties of lettuce and squashes, the intense flavor of the beets and beans, and the large variety of produce. Some struggled with how to use kale and chard but appreciated the weekly supply of onions.

Gardening on the farm has always been a time of solitude, peace, and prayer for me. I usually wake up early in the morning, while it is still cool outside. After my morning coffee and breakfast, I throw on some old clothes, grab my gardening gloves and hat, and head out to the garden. During the walk to the middle of the farm, I enjoy watching the sheep graze out in pasture. Summer chores are minimal for the animals, as long as they stay in the correct pasture paddocks. Once I get to the garden, I first look at all the new growth. Sometimes I pick a few peas, beans, or cherry tomatoes and munch my way through the garden, assessing which areas need the most tending. Most of my morning time in the garden involves pulling weeds, something I don't mind as long as I keep up with them. There aren't many reasons to kill something that's alive and feel good about it. Weeds and mosquitoes are the few exceptions.

Some mornings, I bring the hoe along and hill the beans or manicure around the pepper plants or broccoli. If mulch gets in early enough, the amount of weeding diminishes greatly. Not everything can be mulched, especially plants that attract squash bugs. I learned the hard way that mulch creates a very nice home for squash bugs. When I took away the mulch and added some nasturtiums, I had far fewer problems with them.

The garden gave me quiet time to think and pray. Most days, it was just me and God out in the garden, marveling at His creation. The air was so still and quiet that you could almost hear a pin drop. Imagine my surprise a year earlier when I was out in the garden, hunched low to the ground, weeding quietly, when I heard my husband's voice in the distance. I had been gardening for a few hours and was almost ready to head back to the house. I couldn't see him, but I could hear him clearly, giggling like a little schoolgirl. As I stood up and looked around, I noticed that the wind had picked up from the east, which was a bit unusual, since we usually have the great west winds blow across the state. His voice was getting louder as he got closer, and I heard him say, "How about if you call back after five thirty?" He was talking on his cell phone, and when he saw me, he said, "I can't talk now. I've gotta go." And he hung up the phone.

He was about fifty yards away and walking toward me, as if focused only on me. When he got to the garden gate, I met him and asked, "Who were you talking to on the phone?"

He replied, "Nobody."

I questioned his response. "How could it be nobody when I heard you say to call back after five thirty and you couldn't talk now?" He seemed surprised that I heard anything but flashed a big grin and suggested I was mistaken in what I heard. I was certain of what I clearly heard, and now I was incredibly suspicious. I continued, "It seems odd that you would ask somebody to call back after five thirty when that is the exact time that I need to leave to go to Madison for my meeting tonight." He denied the entire conversation.

What struck me as particularly odd was that, since I had retired two months earlier, he insisted that I write my schedule on the large calendar in the kitchen. Each day, we checked to see what was going on for the day, and I was pretty sure that he had just come from the house, where he would have seen the posting. I didn't know what was going on, buy my gut told me it wasn't normal. I looked at my cell phone and noted the time and date. As soon as I returned to the house, I ran up to the bedroom and recorded it in the back of my prayer journal—Wednesday, July 24, 9:30 a.m.

When I returned to the kitchen on the main floor, I noticed my husband's cell phone sitting in the middle of the kitchen counter. Of course, I opened it to check the call log. The call was deleted.

I started praying for the truth. God knew exactly what was going on, and I counted on Him to reveal to me what I needed to know.

The rest of the day flowed normally. My husband and I worked together; we talked about the store and the farm and ate dinner together. Then promptly at 5:30 p.m., he kissed me good-bye, and I left for Madison to meet a sales rep at seven o'clock in the evening to place product orders for the store through the end of the year. Christmas was a busy time, and I appreciated the effort that the sales rep made to have product samples on display at a hotel so I could see the quality and size of samples before I ordered them. When I arrived at the hotel, I found the conference room with my sales rep, and he told me he was running about twenty minutes behind. He offered me some refreshments and asked me to wait in the lobby while he finished up with another customer. I wasn't hungry, but I had thought of a few last-minute questions about the order that I wanted to discuss with my husband, who was also now my business partner. I called him, and he answered right away but seemed a little surprised and out of breath.

"Are you in the middle of something?" I asked.

"No, why do you ask?" he replied.

"Well, you sound a little winded," I responded. He laughed and asked why I was calling. I told him about the delay and started asking my questions about the order, such as how much was budgeted for this vendor and how early we wanted to take delivery, when I heard shuffling sounds in the background. "Is somebody there?" I asked. He claimed to be alone, but the sounds continued. I knew he was in our house, and we didn't have any pets at the time, since my bullmastiff dog, Elijah, had died just a few months earlier. We talked for about fifteen minutes until the sales rep came to get me. When I got home later that night, everything looked in order but felt strangely different.

The next morning, when I went out to the garden to weed, I prayed for the truth and the strength to deal with whatever the truth revealed. In a few days, we would be heading to Prague for our final European vacation, and though we were traveling with another couple who were friends, I prayed that the trip would be a good time to reconnect with my husband and figure out what was causing the sudden distance between us.

CHAPTER 8

Summer Visitors

I started keeping a guest book inside the yarn shop shortly after it opened. Guests come to visit from all over the country and world. I am blessed to meet interesting and diverse people and always wonder what attracts them to drive out to the farm. Some of the visitors find the store brochure in their hotel or inn; others see it in the local ice cream shop or restaurant. Because the farm is located on a busy state highway, many visitors just pull in the driveway as they drive past. Sometimes that can be hard to do when driving fifty-five miles per hour, so I put painted signs along the road leading up to the driveway, similar to the old Burma Shave signs. The first one is "Yarn Shop Just Ahead," followed by "Organic Seeds," followed by "Wool Fiber," and then "Lamb Meat." I can always remove a sign if the store is out of meat or seeds. I don't think the time will ever come that wool fiber is scarce, since the sheep produce a lot of wool each year and the flock continues to grow.

Most knitters and fiber artists see the "Wool Fiber" sign, slam on the breaks, and swerve into the driveway. Sometimes, their spouses do it on their behalf. Either way, they are always welcome and pleasantly surprised to see the large selection of roving and natural fiber yarns. My sheep have natural colored wool, so many guests marvel at the range of colors produced by nature.

I am fascinated by each person's story and travels. When I ask what brought them to this area, the answers typically include tourism, family visits, or just passing through. Sometimes the same people come back each time they pass through. Parents and grandparents who travel to visit boarding students at a nearby private school can become regular customers for years. When the kids graduate and go off to college, I feel like I'm saying good-bye to a family member when they stop for the last time on graduation weekend.

When I open the store in the morning, I never know who is going to walk through the door. I do pray that I can be a blessing to them. I'll admit that I have to pray that I can be nice to some of them because they don't always walk through the door in a pleasant manner. Most of the time, I feel blessed to have met them after I get to know them. Some visitors become so special that I will never, ever forget them, and I pray for them regularly.

The first summer that I found myself alone on the farm, I started having some extraordinary guests. Little did I know that the "Lamb Meat" sign attracted Muslims to the store. When they inquired about the meat, they weren't satisfied with the large whiteboard listing specific cuts and prices as well as a freezer full of properly inspected, labeled, and packaged lamb chops, roasts, legs, ground lamb, and bratwurst. They wanted a live lamb to kill themselves.

At first, I was appalled. As soon as you walk into the yarn shop, you can see Christian symbols and inspirational gifts. My heritage stems from immigrants who came to this country to escape religious persecution from the King of Prussia back in the 1800s. The ship log for my great-great-great-great-grandfather Gottlieb lists his occupation as a shepherd, and he was one of the first three thousand to head to America to practice their Lutheran religion. I didn't know this until a few years prior when I did more extensive research on my genealogy, but it fit in quite well with what I found myself doing. Behind the main desk and cash register hung a large tapestry of Jesus the Good Shepherd and a flock of sheep. Sophia begged me not to sell anybody a live lamb, and I initially agreed with her.

But I was curious when I started to talk with these special visitors. I asked them what they were going to do with the lamb, how they planned to kill it, and why they felt they needed to do this. Most of the answers varied. One man explained that they used the lamb to feed their extended family and all their neighbors as an act of charity. One gentleman explained that they honored Abraham and his son Ishmael and sacrificed the animal to receive a blessing. One man simply said, "My wife told me I need to bring home a live lamb by Tuesday, and I need to know where I can get one." None of the responses made sense to me, and I typically responded that they didn't need to sacrifice animals anymore, because Jesus came to be the ultimate sacrifice for our sins. At that point, most of them would leave. Some tried to convince me that they knew who Jesus was, but they insisted He wasn't the Son of God but merely a prophet. Regardless of the conversation, I tried hard to give them the good news of Jesus and share that He died for them too, but they usually left disappointed that I wouldn't let them buy a lamb, especially if they could see them grazing outside the store.

This went on for a few months, and other guests in the store who witnessed these encounters seemed to leave with more of an impression than the Muslims. Either way, I felt I planted a seed that the Holy Spirit could nurture and grow into faith.

Along the way, I went to a Sunday-morning Bible study at my church and met a missionary who worked with Muslims in Kazakhstan and Mongolia. I told him about my situation and asked for his advice. He told me, "Sell them a lamb. Animals don't have souls, and nothing in the Bible prohibits animal sacrifice. We don't need to do it because of Christ's sacrifice, but you aren't doing anything wrong by selling them a lamb. Continue to tell them about Jesus, and be sure that each lamb you sell comes with a Bible." This was brilliant and difficult all at the same time. I received a strategy from a Christian man who witnessed Muslims come to faith in Christ and become baptized. But it also meant that I needed to be open to someone who wasn't a professional butcher killing one of my animals. That would be difficult. I trusted God and asked Him to guide me.

The store had a small supply of Bibles. I had once offered a Bible to a man who came into the store. He had dropped his wife off at a local sewing shop and was heading to Cabela's to get some fishing gear. He'd grown up in northern Wisconsin and then lived in Florida. He started making racist comments about Native Americans who fished under treaty in Wisconsin. When I questioned his motives, he proclaimed that he had a right to his opinions and was the subject of reverse discrimination in Florida. He then began making racist remarks about African Americans. He was a guest in my store, and I tried hard to find the right words. The Holy Spirit led me to offer the man a Bible. He replied that he already had one. I asked if he was familiar with the commandment to love his neighbor as himself. He replied that he was tired of taking care of people who refused to provide for themselves and that they were discriminated against because they got what they deserve. I simply said, "Then maybe you should take the Bible to be sure that you don't get what you deserve. Because if I got what I deserved, I would be heading straight to Hades."

The old man looked stunned and replied, "You're not going to Hades, because you're a nice person."

I pushed the Bible toward him and said, "I'm not going to Hades only because Christ died for my sins and erased all of the evil, horrible things I've done in my life. That's what I'm counting on." Speechless, he turned and left the store. I always pray for people after conversations like that because I need God to stir their hearts. He didn't take the Bible, but he did say he had one at home. I hope he opened it and found some comfort there when he returned home. Only God knows what happened after he left.

So I still had a few Bibles left, some New Testament versions and a few with both the Old and New Testaments that my husband had ordered from Gideon and left behind in the store. I never knew when they might come in handy. My husband was an elder in the church and former church chairman. He ushered and served Communion regularly. Most importantly to me, he went to church with me every single Sunday and put his arm around me during the sermon, and we snuggled up in the church pew like honeymooners. When the store opened, I suggested that we use it as an opportunity to witness to people who didn't yet know Christ. I had served on the evangelism and stewardship boards at church and felt called to tell the good news when the opportunity arose. It wasn't really hard to do, since the Holy Spirit did all the work and I just had to be a willing servant and vessel. Sophia was on board with the mission as well. Since I worked more hours in the store, I seemed to be there when God brought special visitors through the door.

One summer afternoon, two young gentlemen walked through the door, looking to buy a live lamb. They looked like they were in their late twenties or early thirties, tall and thin with dark hair and brown skin. They were well dressed and polite and spoke English to me but spoke to each other in a way I couldn't understand. I had a few cull ewes that were going to market later that week and already had their health checked by a vet. I offered the cuts of meat in the freezer, but they insisted on a live animal. I walked outside with them and stood in the store parking lot, showing them the ewes in the adjacent pen that were ready to leave the farm. They didn't mind that they were a few years old and female. When I asked what they planned to do, they explained that they were Muslim and needed one for a blessing.

I told them about Jesus and how He was the ultimate sacrifice and they didn't need to kill animals anymore. But if they wanted one of my sheep, the condition was that it came with a Bible. They looked at each other and starting speaking quietly. I couldn't understand what they were saying, so I stood there patiently and silently waiting for a response. Finally, one of the gentlemen turned to me and asked if he could have a free Bible even if he didn't take the sheep. "Absolutely," I replied. "Let's go back in the store, and I'll get a Bible for you."

When we got back in the store, they waited by the counter as I went to get a New Testament for them. Before I got very far, the second gentleman asked, "Excuse me, but could I please have a free Bible too?"

I could hardly believe my ears. "Yes, of course," I said. I handed each man a Bible, and they thanked me as they left. I prayed for them too.

The next day, a woman from Milwaukee called to inquire about store hours. She wanted to come to the store where she'd heard miracles happen, and she wanted to bring her family. Now, I didn't ask if there was any connection between her and the two gentlemen from the day before, because frankly, that was a confidential matter between them and God. And I didn't ask her what miracles she'd heard had happened at the farm. It didn't really matter to me, since I saw miracles happening almost every day. Later in the day, two carloads of visitors arrived at the store that included parents, children, and grandchildren. They didn't look like they were from the area, so I asked where they were from. They explained that they were visiting the United States from Saudi Arabia and signed the guest book, listing Riyadh as their home city. In my mind, it's a miracle that somebody from Saudi Arabia walked through the doors of my little store on a rural farm. I helped them take pictures of their visit and enjoyed the time I spent with them. I will never forget those two days and what a blessing it was to be chosen by God to witness to those two gentlemen.

When I look back at the guest book now, I see listings over the next few weeks of visitors from Michigan, New York, Ukraine, Russia, Florida, Missouri, North Carolina, Illinois, and Wisconsin. But then I see another remarkable day that started with a visit from a pastor, his wife, and their daughter, Grace. They were traveling back home from vacation and stopped for a little rest break. They were delightful. As they were checking out, a man in his midthirties walked in wearing a suit. He headed toward the honey and started asking questions about why the honey colors were different and where it was harvested, since it was labeled as local.

The pastor's family left, and I was alone with this well-dressed man who then approached the counter. He wanted to buy a jar of honey but also wanted to know about buying a live lamb. He explained that he was an immigration attorney from Chicago and was visiting a client at the county jail, which is about four miles from the farm. He added that he went to law school at the University of Wisconsin and usually headed back to Chicago through Madison so he could stop to visit. He had no idea why he headed home in a different direction that day but was pleasantly surprised to see the "Lamb Meat" sign. I told him that live lambs came with a Bible and that he wouldn't be able to take a lamb that day because they needed to be checked by a vet within thirty days of being sold or butchered. He said that would be fine because he didn't want to transport a live animal back to Chicago in his $80,000 car. But then he started asking me questions. "What language were the books of the New Testament written in?"

I told him I didn't know, but it didn't really matter to me because they were all God's words, regardless of the language used. He then told me that he was Muslim and that at the end of time, his god would be first and my God, who was first in this world, would be last—and that was written in Scripture. I almost started laughing and grabbed a Bible to find the passage he was mistakenly trying to quote. I said, "That is not what is written in Scripture."

But when I reached for the New Testament to give him, he became angry and yelled at me. "I don't want that little Bible! I want the whole Bible." I told him that would be fine and handed him the Bible with the complete Old and New Testaments. At that moment, my father-in-law walked in the store and heard the commotion. The attorney held up the Bible and yelled again, "I will pray for the truth, and then I will be back."

I have no idea why the Holy Spirit gave me these words, but I said, "I will be praying for the truth too, and my God, who is the God of truth, will answer my prayers for you. I look forward to seeing you again."

My father-in-law stood there in disbelief. "What was that all about?" he asked. I summarized the visit for him, and he said he would be praying too. At that exact moment, one of my CSA customers walked through the door. This person happened to be a member of the prayer chain at my father-in-law's church. I recounted the story and asked if she would pray for this man too and if she could have the entire prayer chain pray for him. She responded that their church had a new policy and needed a specific name in order to submit a prayer request.

"Well, God knows which Chicago attorney came into the yarn shop today and walked out with a Bible," I replied. "I'm sure he is the only one who fits that description." But she insisted she couldn't help without a name.

As we stood there chatting about what produce was in the bag that week, my father-in-law left the store to return home. The conversation soon covered other topics beyond produce, and eventually, the CSA customer decided it was time to head home too. As she turned to leave, she stooped down and picked up a crumpled piece of paper from the floor. She handed me the paper wad and said, "Here's some garbage that someone dropped, if you want to throw it away." I thanked her and opened the paper to see what it was. To my surprise, it clearly belonged to the Chicago attorney. He had dropped a phone message from his office with his name clearly printed on the top.

I handed the paper back to her and said, "Here is the attorney's name. Can you please add him to the prayer list at your church?" We were both amazed. But once she had the name, she didn't need the piece of paper. I still have that phone message slip. I then e-mailed the pastor who was leaving the store when the attorney walked in and asked him to include the man in prayers at his church. He replied back that he would gladly do it.

A Day on the Farm

A few minutes later, a middle-aged couple walked in the store from Pocahontas, Iowa. The man asked how my day was going, and I couldn't contain myself. I had to share the amazing news with him. He then told me he was also a pastor and would pray for this man too.

The attorney hasn't returned to the store yet, but I continue to pray for him and hope to meet him again someday. Hopefully, I will see him in heaven at the feet of my Lord and Savior, Jesus Christ. What a happy day that would be if he could be there with me.

My God is amazing and wonderful. I started to feel like He was showing me His purpose for my life, and I felt humbled and honored. Just a year earlier, I was preparing to walk through the deepest, darkest valley of my life and didn't imagine I could have lived through it. In fact, I had prayed to not live through it, but each morning that I woke up, I asked God to give me the strength to get through another day.

CHAPTER 9

The Fall

The vacation to Prague the year before with my husband was beautiful but strained. The sightseeing was tremendous, the beer was the best I'd ever had, and our friends provided extra laughter along the way. But when I was alone with my husband at the hotel, I knew something serious was going on. I brought my Bible along, did my daily devotion in the Word, and kept praying for the truth. Within a few months, God would answer my prayers.

When we returned to the farm from Prague, our marriage started declining. I had just retired, and we certainly had transition issues to work around with me being on the farm all day, every day. But the easy things became harder, and simple routines such as eating meals together became less frequent. The more I wanted to talk about our issues, the more my husband deflected the topic and blamed me, insinuating that my employment change caused all the problems between us. Satan certainly wanted me to believe that, but I now know it was a huge lie.

I continued going to my weekly Bible study, and the twelve-week session we were about to start happened to include a section on discernment by the Holy Spirit and hearing God speak to our hearts. I knew I needed this. As I did my daily devotions, Scripture called out to me, but I didn't know why at the time. One day, I simply wrote in my prayer journal, "Psalm 37." When I read those words now, they seem almost prophetic, but I didn't know it at the time. I kept praying for the truth and waiting on the Lord. I also kept waiting for the phone bill to come to check the call on July 24. I wasn't expecting much, because our cell phone bills had summarized listings of calls, with all incoming calls simply listing the time of the call and the word "Incoming." I would only be able to see the specific phone numbers of outgoing calls and hoped maybe there would be a listing for five thirty that evening.

I kept busy with the garden and the store. The distance between my husband and I increased, and I noticed he started making himself cocktails several times a week instead of the usual drink or two reserved for special occasions. Finally, in mid-September, the phone bill arrived, weeks later than usual. The envelope was huge, and when I opened it, I found about eighteen pages of detailed listings of phone numbers. A note on the front stated that the cell phone company had just completed a major software upgrade and apologized that all customers received preferred statements because of an unexpected glitch. To my surprise, these more detailed statements contained the phone number of every single incoming call, unlike the statements we had received for the previous eight years. I retrieved my prayer journal and found the entry from the garden. I looked at the number and wrote it down. I also noticed the same number call again several times during the day and again at five thirty. I scanned the listings and found the same number called multiple times a day throughout the month. When I cross-referenced the days with the calendar, the calls only showed up when I was out of town or at appointments.

I said nothing to my husband when the bill arrived, but one day while he showered, I checked his cell phone directory to find out if the number was listed. It was listed under the name of our church organist and cleric. That was odd. Why would that be a secret? As a church elder, it seemed plausible that he might have church business with another church worker. But the conversation I overheard in the garden certainly didn't sound like a business or church-related conversation. The only way to find out would be to ask.

The church organist and cleric looked to be in his late fifties, portly and bald. He and his wife of thirty-two years had three grown children, and I knew enough about him that I couldn't make a connection between his interests and my husband. They didn't play basketball or go to the gym together. The suggestion that we should have dinner with them sometime never materialized. I knew his wife, a nurse, by name and face only. She seemed pleasant and friendly, but our paths never really crossed.

"Why would the cleric call you several times a day, but only on days that I wasn't home?" I asked my husband. He looked surprised but denied the accusation. I then pulled out the phone bill, and his face went blank. I continued, "I have never given my schedule to the cleric. How would he know when I was away?" He recovered quickly and replied that he chose to talk about church business when I wasn't around because he then had uninterrupted time.

"Does he come out to the house to visit?" I asked. This concerned me greatly, since Sophia worked at the store, and the house cleanliness left a lot to be desired. I would have been embarrassed for an unexpected guest to see the untidiness. My husband replied emphatically that the cleric had never stepped foot in our house.

Things didn't add up. I know what I heard in the garden, and my gut told me instantly that this was a lie. I was surprised that I didn't even know my husband had any church business relating to the music program and even more surprised that if something as innocent as church business was going on with these calls, then they wouldn't need to be secretly deleted from his phone log.

I called a friend, who suggested I trust my gut. At that point, I thought he either had a false name attached to the phone number or the cleric was covering for my husband's extramarital affair. Either way, my husband kept a secret that I didn't know. Until I had answers, I moved out of our bedroom and into a guest room. My husband's drinking escalated, but I didn't get any answers. I did get direction from God, who led me to specific Scriptures in my devotions. God gave me devotions on secret sins, wolves in sheep's clothing, and flattering lips that are filled with deceit. God also gave me passages from the book of Amos on speaking up and words of encouragement that He would never leave me and would protect me from evil.

As I look back at my prayer journal, I see how He was working to prepare me for the truth. I prayed for my husband, truth, and repentance. I loved this man very much, and it hurt me to see him struggle almost as much as his secrets were hurting me. I shared my quarterly devotional booklet with him and asked if he wanted to do daily devotions with me. That never happened.

The quarterly voter's meeting was scheduled at church later in September, and calling the cleric as a third pastor to serve the congregation appeared on the agenda. Our church, like many other churches, struggled financially. Many congregational members questioned the soundness of adding staff when we struggled to keep the church school open. As we drove to the voter's meeting, I asked my husband if he thought the cleric would make a good pastor. He laughed and said, "Absolutely not."

I already planned to vote against the cleric's calling simply because of his involvement with my husband's schemes and lies. After much discussion about calling a third pastor, the vote was taken. Some people requested a secret ballot, but the chairperson didn't think it was necessary. I, along with a few others, voted against it. Surprisingly, my husband voted for it. As we left the church, I was stunned. We walked past the cleric, who nervously waited in the narthex. My husband smiled broadly at him, shook his hand, and congratulated him on the successful vote. "Why would you vote in favor of calling the cleric when you just told me that you didn't think he was fit to be a pastor?" I asked in total disbelief when we got back in the car.

"Because he has worked so hard the past four years preparing through the seminary, I felt like he deserved it," my husband replied.

The next morning, I scheduled an appointment with one of the pastors to discuss the phone bill and see if the church knew about the frequent and odd phone calls supposedly discussing church business. I couldn't get in until later in the week. When I arrived at the church office, the pastor was behind closed doors with another parishioner. I waited, phone bill in hand. To my surprise, my father-in-law walked out, smiling and cheery. He had no idea there were any issues between me and his son. He didn't ask why I was there and apparently never mentioned it to anyone else.

I was nervous to meet with the pastor. My disclosure to him shed light on a huge secret, but I had no idea what it was. I calmly explained that I didn't think I could continue to be a member at a congregation with a new pastor that held some secret information about my husband. I showed him the phone records—page after page of call details that showed dozens of calls between the two over the past few months. His face went white. He told me that he wasn't aware of any church business between the two of them and didn't even know they were friends. I asked to transfer to another church in the area. He assured me that he would get the paperwork ready to complete the transfer, and there was nothing more that needed to be done on my part. My transfer would be presented to the board of elders the following month, and since I was a member in good standing, there shouldn't be any objection.

When I told my husband about the pending transfer, he became upset about what other people in the congregation would think and ask. "Then tell me the truth about what is going on," I begged. He refused. I talked with my friend again and gave her an update on what was happening. She suggested that I reach out to the cleric's wife to find out if she knew anything. Since I didn't really know Kate, I looked at that as a last resort. How would I approach her about something so bizarre?

In the meantime, I continued helping my father-in-law with estate issues from my mother-in-law's death in May. My mother-in-law was like a sister to me, and I missed her dearly. If she were still alive, she would have found the answers for me. She taught kindergarten at the church school for decades and was beloved by her students. She was an incredibly generous soul who loaned people money whenever she could help. She paid for students' hot lunches when their parents got behind. She helped pay tuition bills and field trip fees for families she knew needed extra help. When she passed away, my father-in-law found money in coat pockets and drawers and gift certificates in thank you cards throughout the house. To show his appreciation for my help, he gave me some of his findings, including a twenty-dollar gift certificate to the local diner. As much as I missed my mother-in-law, my friendship with my father-in-law grew. He was lonely and stopped by the store almost every day. He started coming to Thursday night knit nights and read Louis L'Amour western stories aloud while we knit. He came over to dinner often but left as soon as the meal was finished so that he wouldn't overstay his welcome.

As much as I wanted to share my discoveries with him, I couldn't. He needed to heal from his grief and didn't need any more distress. Yet I didn't want him to be surprised when he went to the elder meeting and wondered why I was transferring to another congregation. I prayed about that too.

Shortly after I met with the pastor, he drove out to the farm to see me. It was a CSA day, and I was busy getting produce in from the garden. I was quite surprised to see him so early in the morning, but I could tell it was urgent. "I have some news to share with you," he started. "The cleric has resigned from his position, and I just finished helping him pack up his office and move out before the rest of the office staff arrived for work. The cleric has also asked to transfer out of the congregation. Would you please reconsider transferring your membership?"

I asked why he resigned so abruptly but was told it was a confidential matter. I hoped it wasn't because of my phone report, and he assured me it wasn't. But he did want to talk to my husband because he thought he might have some useful information. As we were talking at the back door, my husband approached hurriedly from wherever he had been on the farm. He smiled nervously and said, "Well, hello, Pastor. What brings you out here so early in the morning?"

Pastor shared the news of the cleric resigning and asked if my husband knew anything about it. My husband feigned surprise, said he didn't know anything, and the pastor left.

We went out for a Friday fish fry a few nights later at one of our favorite spots. Even though my husband suggested the date night out, he didn't say much. In the twenty minutes that we waited for our fish orders, he ordered and drank three large old-fashioned cocktails. I drove the two of us home, and we went to bed in our separate beds.

I knew I needed to talk with Kate, the cleric's wife. Why would the pastor drive out specifically to talk with me and think my husband may know something if there wasn't some connection between the two?

In the meantime, another family member was diagnosed with metastatic cancer and faced a lot of uncertainty. Maybe a nurse's perspective would be helpful. I prayed until one night, I finally got the courage to call Kate. Either she would meet with me or she wouldn't. But I wouldn't know if I didn't ask. I looked in the church directory for their home number, dialed, and the cleric answered the phone. I asked to speak with Kate, and he said she had just walked in the door from work. Then he asked who was calling. I couldn't lie or make him suspicious, so I simply stated my name, to which he replied, "Oh!"

Kate took the phone from him and cheerfully greeted me. "Well, that was perfect timing. I just walked through the door, and I still have my coat on."

"Well, I'm glad I caught you. I won't keep you long. I was wondering if you would like to have coffee with me some morning," I stated. I explained that it would be a treat from my late mother-in-law and that twenty dollars would probably cover a light breakfast too. I explained about the medical diagnosis and wanted to get her perspective on what to expect. She suggested we meet the next morning since that was her day off. Relieved, I agreed.

We met at the local diner the next morning and sat in a corner booth. She was embarrassed about her husband's resignation and didn't want to be near any of the town gossips who gathered for their daily kaffeeklatsch.

Pleasant and cheery, Kate and I reminisced about my mother-in-law. Their children enjoyed having her as a kindergarten teacher, and we all missed her. I asked about cancer found in the bones, and she suggested tests that might be helpful. By the second cup of coffee, the topic turned to church business, and she disclosed that her husband resigned after they discovered explicit material on their home computer. Now I was even more curious about the connection with my husband. I told her about the pastor's visit and how my husband claimed he didn't know anything about the resignation. Kate suggested that might be true, but she really didn't know who all knew about it. "But then, why would your husband be calling my husband several times a day, several times a month, but only when I'm not home?" I inquired.

"Well, because they're good friends!" she exclaimed. "He comes out to the farm all the time!"

"What?" I blurted. "He told me your husband has never stepped foot in our house."

Kate's face looked alarmed. "Oh, no. He's been going out there for years."

"Then why would he lie to me about all of this?" I asked. I was confused. But Kate had a very strong suspicion that she knew what was going on. She told me she needed to go talk with the pastor but would be in touch with me later that afternoon.

I returned to open the store, and my husband came through the back door to find out what took so long when I went to town in the morning. I looked right at him and said, "I met Kate for breakfast, and you are such a big liar." At that point, I only knew that he lied about the cleric visiting the farm frequently.

But he looked right back at me, flashed a big grin, and said, "You can't prove anything!" He turned and left the store.

Now I was extremely rattled. Fear gripped me, and my hands started shaking. I felt like throwing up. "Dear God, what is going on?" I asked out loud.

I paced. I waited on customers. Time felt like an eternity. Shortly after noon, Kate called and asked if she could come to the store to talk with me in person. By the time she arrived, she told me that the pastor would be there shortly. I had customers in the store and tried to hurry their yarn selections. I doubt they sensed my inner panic, because they took a very long time to choose the exact right yarn. I remained pleasant and pulled together even as the pastor arrived in his red pickup truck. I could see him talking with Kate outside, and he looked concerned. After the last customer left, the two of them came in and asked me to sit down.

Kate started first. When she got home at noon, her husband was there along with two of their children. She firmly asked the cleric what exactly had been going on with my husband. Since he knew she had just come from coffee with me and that their marriage was already on the line, he blurted out many of the gory details. He described what they did, where they did it, and how often they got together. I learned that he had been in my house and living room, as well as the store and many other places. I don't think he really cared how tidy my house was because that's not what was on their minds.

The pastor summarized what she was saying because my mind went numb. "Your husband has been having a sexual affair with the cleric for an extended period of time," he said. He added that infidelity certainly was a biblical reason for divorce, and he would understand if that's the route I decided to take.

I couldn't think. I sat there frozen, trying to sort things out. I had no idea where my husband went after he left the store in the morning, but I was pretty sure he wasn't at the farm. The pastor asked me not to confront my husband about any of this and that he wanted to do it personally. He asked me to go up to the house, get any guns, and bring them to him. If I was asked why, I was supposed to say that the pastor had offered to clean them before hunting season. With his military background, that seemed plausible at the time. He then asked me to make arrangements to go away for the weekend and not return until he called me to let me know it was okay. After he left the store, he went to my father-in-law's house to retrieve any guns stored there.

I had prayed for the truth, and now I had it—or at least part of it—but this wasn't what I wanted to hear. How was it even comprehensible that these two church leaders who served Communion together on Sunday morning were having an affair on the side? Pain seared my heart when I thought about my husband putting his arm around me every Sunday during the church sermon while the organist sat a few feet away, watching. I was disgusted by the extreme betrayal and afraid of the future between us.

As soon as the pastor left, I called my daughter, Liz, and asked if I could stay with her for a few days. She had a one-bedroom apartment near Lake Michigan, and I needed a safe place to go. She had wanted me to help her with a few things, and I needed to pick up some sheepskins from the tannery in Milwaukee, so the excuse wouldn't seem so unusual when I told my husband about my plans. Liz was incredibly sympathetic, though I never wanted to lean on my children to be my caretakers. I'm sure she wondered how long I planned to stay when I carried up my luggage. People do strange things when they are in a state of shock. It looked like I had packed enough to last the winter. I threw in clothes, my Bible and devotional materials, about fifteen knitting projects, and five pairs of shoes. What was I thinking? It truly was a blur.

Liz graciously cared for me. She gave me her bed and slept on the couch. She cooked for me, took me on long walks along the lakefront, and reassured me that I would be okay. The next day, Kate called my cell phone to let me know that her children, who had overheard the whole disclosure from their dad, had already started telling some of their friends, and she couldn't control who would find out. The pastor called me after he met with my husband, who initially denied the affair. When faced with the irrefutable truth, however, he reluctantly admitted part of what was going on. My husband then called me and begged me to come home. I agreed to return if he promised to tell me the truth about what had happened. He agreed to the stipulation, but that was another lie.

When I returned home, my husband helped me unload the sheepskins and asked if we could go to the Saturday evening church service. He looked incredibly distraught, so I agreed. After church, he met with the pastor, and we picked up take-out Chinese food on the way home. During dinner, it hit me. One never knows when an emotional tidal wave is coming, but it hits hard. I started crying uncontrollably. My husband did absolutely nothing to comfort me. He sat there and continued to eat his dinner. When I could finally speak, I told him I needed to go upstairs to calm down and wanted to talk with him in a few minutes. He said nothing. When I came back downstairs fifteen minutes later, the house was dark. His keys, wallet, and cell phone were on the counter, and he was gone, but all the vehicles were still there. It was pitch black outside, so I went out into the darkness and started calling for him. He chose to stay in the darkness and never responded.

Fearing the worst, I called my son, Jim. I was crying uncontrollably again, and he offered to call the pastor to come out to the house. The pastor showed up with help and was visibly shaken. He promised to find my husband no matter what and asked me to stay in the house. Within the hour, Pastor came back to tell me they found him safe. He was sleeping on the couch in the store. When I asked my husband why he left without leaving a note or saying anything, he simply responded that he was tired and wanted to sleep and didn't want to listen to my crying. I went to bed relieved that he was unharmed, but I felt mentally exhausted.

On Sunday morning, I got a cup of coffee and asked if we could sit down and talk. He said, "Sure." He then proceeded to talk about purchasing thousands of dollars of lime to spread on one of the farms before a hard frost set in.

I looked at him incredulously. "Why would we invest money in a farm that we might not own next year?"

He looked at me, totally confused about why that would be an issue. "You're not thinking about divorcing me, are you?"

I couldn't believe what I was hearing. My world had just been ripped apart. I just found out that the man I married was living a secret life, all the while pretending to be a devoted husband and church leader. While he encouraged me to retire, he lied to me about his commitment to our future together. Now, when the time came for him to tell me the truth, to ask me to forgive him and show even an ounce of remorse, he came up empty. I looked at him and said, "That option is still on the table if we can't work things out."

The pastor asked my husband to move out of the house for two weeks to give me some time to think, and we spent the day making arrangements. I called Kate to make sure he wouldn't end up at the same hotel as the cleric. When he finally left, I felt a huge sense of relief. I needed the quiet time to think, pray, and rest as best I could. We decided that Sophia or I would be the only workers in the store from this point on because of the scandal, and that would require more of my time.

I walked around in a fog for a few days. I just couldn't wrap my head around something that seemed so unbelievable. How could I not have known he was gay? He insisted he wasn't. He also insisted he wasn't bisexual. I talked with some close trusted friends from other states, and they expressed shock and disbelief. Nobody saw this coming at all.

Instead of being truthful for the first time in our marriage, my husband continued to lie. He didn't stay at the hotel for two weeks. He snuck into one of the outbuildings and slept on the floor. When I asked him to return to the hotel, he refused and started sleeping in his truck out on the marsh in freezing temperatures at night. In hindsight, he may have hoped that I would feel sorry for him and let him move back in the house. He refused to find suitable housing, so the pastor and I secured a small apartment with a month-to-month lease.

Within a few weeks, my husband told me that he wasn't gay; he was a sex addict. I had never heard of the term, but he planned to go to a Christian-based healing workshop in Tennessee to deal with his issues. He still had primary responsibility for the animals but sometimes wouldn't show up to care for them when he said he would. This did nothing to help rebuild trust with me. I was shattered, my father-in-law was devastated, and the church poured all their energy into helping my husband. Instead of asking him to resign as a church elder, they allowed him to take a leave of absence. They refused to process my membership transfer because they didn't want to draw attention to the situation. The church never once offered help for me or my children, though we were all members in good standing. One day, the pastor came to talk to me about how important it would be for me to stay married. I burst into tears and ran out of the store. My father-in-law walked in during the meeting and offered to stay in the store until I could regain my composure. We were both betrayed and hurt by the same man.

I called the pastor at the church I wanted to attend and asked if he could expedite the transfer process. He couldn't believe how this was being handled and offered to help in any way he could. I wrote a letter directly to the chairperson of the board of elders and asked to be released. The effort the church went through to try to protect my husband couldn't be matched by the wildfire created by the town gossips. Within days, I received a call from a dear friend whose husband had heard all about my husband's affair at the Legion hall, along with crass jokes about what they supposed had happened at the farm. The people making the comments were close personal friends of the senior pastor and some of the elders. I had to confirm to her that portions of the story actually were true, and she was shocked at how quickly my life changed and the tremendous problems I now faced. She asked what I was going to do. I told her I had no idea.

Though I asked to be left alone, my husband left notes and letters in my car. He was sorry that I had to find out about what happened. He also shared information about other men, other sexual contact, and how he prayed for a miracle to save our marriage. I started reading about sex addiction and encouraged him to get help. I knew and admired many people who overcame drug and alcohol addictions and hoped he could do the same. But I had no control over his sobriety. Sophia and her church offered to help, and I knew that with God, nothing was impossible.

When my husband left for the sex addiction conference, I took over the care of the animals and was shocked at how thin the alpacas looked. I immediately started giving them grain and took an orphaned baby alpaca, or cria, named Naomi into the house because she was so weak she couldn't even stand up. My new pastor came to meet with me and bless the house. He seemed surprised to see Naomi in the whirlpool bathtub. He went through each room in the house with me, offering prayers and readings and following a service to restore authority over my home, store, and farm back to the triune God. He also referred me to a reputable therapist to help me deal with the wreckage I faced.

Since I had to take charge of the animals for a week, I moved the thin alpacas up to the lambing barn, where they would stay warmer. I noticed that Rose, the oldest llama, shivered constantly. I called the vet to come to the farm and check the animals. She came right away and provided tips and pointers on how to help the alpacas and llamas. She owned several llamas herself and offered a wealth of information. Llamas need access to tepid water in winter, and I needed a tank heater to keep the ice off the top of the stock tank. I found a portable electric tank heater, brand-new and still in the box, on a shelf in the basement. Naomi, who had been orphaned when she was a few weeks old, returned to the barn when she was strong enough to stand. But she remained incredibly small and thin. I tried giving her milk replacer in a bottle while she rested in my whirlpool bathtub, but she wouldn't take a bottle. The vet suggested that I try a bottle with one of the other crias to see if that would help Naomi not be afraid to try it. I moved Trinity, the other cria, into the pen with Naomi and found that Trinity loved drinking milk from a bottle!

Naomi remained disinterested. So then Trinity decided she would drink both bottles, chewing on my jacket sleeve until I relented and gave her Naomi's bottle too. The vet also suggested trying the milk in a flat pan on the barn floor to see if Naomi would drink it like she drank water. Naomi still resisted, but the farm cats loved the extra treat.

In addition to trying to get extra nourishment and calories into Naomi, the vet strongly encouraged putting 100 percent wool sweaters on the crias. I went to the local thrift store and found a few sweaters, including a vintage Pendleton sweater in size extra-small for Naomi. I cut the sleeves out of the sweaters and put them on the babies. They looked cute, and I saw firsthand the difference it made in keeping them warm. They needed to use every ounce of energy to grow instead of trying so hard to stay warm in the below-zero temperatures.

Naomi wears her vintage Pendleton wool sweater to keep warm.

A Day on the Farm

When my husband returned from the conference, he disclosed additional information to let me know that his addiction had been a problem for most of his life, but he was committed to working on it. He thought it would be important for me to attend the upcoming Partners of Sex Addicts conference at the same facility, because he expected that I needed to make some changes too.

Sophia watched the store for a week while I headed to Nashville. I learned a lot about sex addiction and met some amazing women who were dealing with the same issues I faced. When we got together and shared our stories the first day, the pain in the room was palpable. Though the counselor who worked with us emphasized how much time I needed to heal from this incredible trauma, I was surprised that no guidelines were offered on how that should happen. Most of the conference focused on understanding sex addiction and the sex addict.

I learned three critical pieces of information at the conference. One session on tolerance described the brain's chemical reaction to sex addiction as being very similar to drug and alcohol addiction. Drug addicts don't usually start by shooting up heroin, and sex addicts usually don't start their first sexual encounters having same-sex experiences. As tolerance develops, new experiences have to be more extreme in order for the addict to get high. The next steps on the tolerance continuum were all criminal offenses. In fact, many sex addicts do end up incarcerated if they don't continue with treatment.

The second critical piece of information related to reconciliation. The first step to possible marriage reconciliation required full disclosure by the sex addict. I had a right to know every single instance of sexual acting out since the day we married. Without full disclosure, there was no hope for a marriage to be rebuilt. As I looked back at our marriage, I could recall specific, suspicious incidents when I thought something was going on but my husband charismatically reassured me that nothing was wrong and pledged his undying love to me. At this point, he had disclosed only pieces of information but wouldn't answer all the questions I had.

The third critical piece of information I received was that my husband had a lot of hard work to do in order to overcome his addiction. Intensive individual therapy, complete transparency, couples therapy, and regular attendance at Sex Addicts Anonymous (SAA) meetings would be critical. This was a battle my husband would fight every day for the rest of his life, and the risk of relapse was so high that the Partners of Sex Addicts conference actually had a session on how to handle relapses. The issue wasn't even if a relapse would happen but what to do when it happened.

The bonds I forged with these other wives fighting the same demons in their husbands will last forever. I still keep in touch with them, and the ones I hear from are all still married. Some of their husbands got on their knees and begged for forgiveness, and they now cherish marriage as the precious gift that God intended it to be. The process of going through full disclosure and setting up accountability measures was hard for them, but their husbands were willing to do anything necessary to save their relationships. God truly can work miracles when we put our trust in Him, turn from the darkness, and truly seek the light He offers.

I called my husband before I left the conference and told him what I learned and what would be necessary for reconciliation. I needed time to heal, and he needed to disclose everything that happened during our marriage. That wasn't the message he hoped to hear.

The change of scenery helped me tremendously, and I returned to the store refreshed, hopeful, and reenergized. I wasn't expecting the next revelation, but sometimes God shows us things that we need to know for our benefit. I continually prayed for protection from evil, and what I saw on the store computer truly shocked me.

The first day back in the store was cold and snowy. I looked for a knitting pattern that a customer had inquired about before I left and couldn't find it. I knew that it was on a vendor's website that I had seen before I left, so I opened the computer browsing history. There I found page after page of sex-related websites and news articles about sexually violent and criminal behavior. Emotionally, I lost it. I became physically nauseated.

I picked up the phone and called my husband. I read each line and asked why he was in the store and using business equipment to feed his addiction. He denied being in the store or on the computer. He and Sophia were the only people who had keys to the store besides me, and I had been out of state. He continued to deny he had anything to do with it. I then told him I would simply print the browsing history off and send it to his therapist. He finally admitted he was responsible and begged me not to print it off. I knew at that moment there was little hope of saving our marriage. It wasn't the problem with his weak flesh, because we all struggle with temptation and sin. The problem was his allegiance to the father of lies and unwillingness to submit to God.

I knew that my firm stand against evil meant I would potentially have to leave his family's farm, but I needed to put God first in my life, not my husband, and this was a line I wouldn't cross. I eventually found the knitting pattern and printed it off. I then downloaded the application to do mission work in Prague and arranged to meet with my pastors. But clearly, God wasn't ready for me to leave the farm just yet.

CHAPTER 10

Spiritual Warfare

Shortly after the first Muslim visitors came to the farm and the Holy Spirit worked through me to give them Bibles, I needed to meet with my banker to finalize the refinancing of the farm in order to stay long-term. Having spent most of my career in the financial services industry, I knew the bleak prospect of obtaining a loan in my own name. My credit rating was strong, but I no longer had the income from the year before, when I had retired. Through the blessings of the T-shirt fundraiser, several hundred dollars could be put toward the cause. One of my meat customers, a professional photographer, generously donated photos he took on the farm for use in the farm calendar. The calendars had just arrived, but I needed to sell quite a few just to make up the initial printing costs. I checked into low-interest government loans for farmers, loans for women small business owners, and conventional financing. Most of the programs had loan limits of up to $300,000. I needed a loan for $740,000. I couldn't get any of the numbers to work. According to my calculations, I couldn't afford to stay.

A Day on the Farm

I called my good friend, Joni, in Dallas. We became friends when God put us together in a hotel room in St. Louis, randomly assigned by alphabetical listing, to attend financial services training a decade ago. That became one of God's most amazing interventions in my life because she became a trusted confidant and sister to me. From a human perspective, the numbers don't add up. In her Texas drawl, Joni bluntly said, "First of all, y'all need to understand it's not your farm. It's God's farm, and He chose you to manage it. God can make the payments. And you need to let Him work it out."

With that encouragement, I put together my organic farming plan and went to meet with the banker. I presented my case and gave him the detailed income statement and balance sheet of assets and debts as well as projected income. He looked it over carefully, leaned back in his chair, and crossed his arms. I prepared for the anticipated rejection. He said, "I'm familiar with your situation, and I will approve your loan today. I have the authority to approve it, so we don't have to take it to the bank board. We'll need to take care of a few details, like a copy of the most recent appraisal, but we can schedule the closing in as soon as a week or two." He then asked for my e-mail address so he could put the commitment in writing. He went over the quarterly payment structure for the note and then added, "If you ever have trouble making the payments, please come and talk with me so I can help you figure out a solution."

Once the title was transferred to me, we planned a huge open house for the store, complete with Sophia, Liz, Jim, and Kristina. Kristina painted a sheep cover for her favorite bottle lamb, number eighty-nine, to wear with the words "Support Our Farm; Buy a Calendar." He was adorable and effective with his walking billboard. All the lambs grazed in the pasture next to the store. Customers loved watching them and seeing how much they had grown over the summer. A friend brought her spinning wheel business to set up under a tent outside and gave demonstrations. We served up lamb bratwurst samples, and God blessed us with beautiful weather.

We planned for the future. We honored the Lord by closing the store on Sundays, and I looked forward to having one day off each week. Jim got some marking paint and located all the points to add new posts, gates, and higher fencing to facilitate rotational grazing for the sheep. He somehow got his college roommate to agree to help install all the fencing over Labor Day weekend. The future looked very bright.

Shortly after the open house, without any warning, one of the lambs got sick. He was out grazing in the pasture one day, and the next day, he could barely stand up and walk. I moved him up to the lambing barn, and within hours, he was dead. I called the vet, and she suggested it might be a selenium deficiency because of the poor soil. I called Jim, and he drove two and a half hours to bury the dead lamb for me, as it was too heavy for me to carry. He helped me give shots of BO-SE, a special selenium and Vitamin E mineral supplement, to every adult sheep and lamb on the farm. I was thankful for his help and hoped this solved the problem.

Little number eighty-nine fell over dead a few days later. I checked the flock and noticed two more lambs barely able to walk. I moved them up to the lambing barn and called the vet to come and do some tests. She withdrew some blood and took a fecal sample. It took a few days to get results. Both lambs died by the time she called to say they found nothing significant other than a few roundworms. Each meat animal was worth about $300, and I prayed that God would heal them and help me figure out how to take care of them before more of them got sick. I checked my shepherd books and went online for answers, but nothing seemed to match what was happening. I started feeding them really good hay in case the pasture wasn't dense enough in nutrients.

My friend, Joni, sent me two books on spiritual warfare. I started reading them and couldn't make the connection. I talked with one of my pastors who stopped in the store to visit. He said, "Look around the store. You have a target on your back. You are proclaiming the Word of Christ here."

Of course Satan knew who I was and what I was trying to do. He was ramping up the war to get me to stop. He was trying to wear me down and get me to quit. Another lamb died, and I was exasperated. I got on my knees and prayed that God would help me, just like He always had. I knew God could heal the lambs, and I knew He would point me to the answers I needed. What was the lesson He was trying to teach me? I had to turn everything over to Him and trust that He would show me His wisdom.

The state veterinarian planned to come to the farm to do his annual flock inspection within the week. He had extensive experience with sick sheep, specifically scrapie, but maybe this was the resource I needed to figure things out. The state vet typically only checked all the sheep more than fourteen months of age, but I thought it would be a great opportunity to see if he could help me. I got my questions ready and waited for his arrival. Another lamb died before inspection day.

I noticed that one of the Bibles that had been donated to the store had a large sword on the cover and was titled *God's Victorious Army Bible: Spiritual Warfare Reference Edition*. I picked it up and started reading. I could hardly put it down. I took it up to the house at night and read some more. I learned about the power of speaking God's Word and Christ's blood to defeat Satan. I realized I lived in the middle of a spiritual battlefield. But I also learned that my God always wins! I knew that Christ already defeated death and the Devil. I started looking at Satan as a nuisance to me rather than a threat. And he had no power over God's plan for me and the farm. God had already started showing me how He could turn destruction into glory, and I fully trusted God's power and timing.

Everything went well on inspection day. The state vet complimented me on the good health of the animals. I told him all about the lambs that had died, and he concurred with the protocol I'd followed. He couldn't think of any biological reason that they should suddenly fall over dead. Part of the inspection involves a physical accounting of each animal and its flock identification number. Every adult animal matched his identification records, appeared healthy to him, and he signed the official report. I signed the report, took my copy, and put the file away for another year.

I started giving good hay to the ewes to supplement the dwindling pasture and begin preparing them for breeding, which would start in a few weeks, right after shearing. I routinely counted them each day to be sure a straggler wasn't still out in pasture. Two days after the flock inspection, I noticed a sheep was missing. I counted them again and came up one short. I headed toward the pasture to find the lost sheep but didn't get far. A ewe stood in the cool shade behind the barn, her ears pointing down. She was only a few years old with beautiful brown wool. As I approached her, she stood still and didn't move. I checked her over, and nothing seemed apparent. She certainly wasn't injured or stuck. But she didn't look well. I ran to the house to grab a syringe and dose of penicillin. When I returned, she fell over dead before my eyes. As I stood there, looking at my beautiful dead ewe, a fire raged within me. I looked up to the heavens, held up my arms, and screamed at the top of my lungs, "Satan, get off my farm. By the blood of Jesus Christ, I command you and all your minions to leave right now and never, ever come back! You have no authority here!"

I called the state veterinarian and told him about the ewe that fell over dead. He was shocked and arranged to come and sever the head to take to the state lab for testing. I got Bob and hauled the carcass down to the burial ground. The test results came back normal.

But no more animals died.

CHAPTER 11

Off to Market

The lambs soon grew big enough to go to market. Customers called the store for weeks, anxiously waiting for their grass-fed lamb meat. I still didn't have a livestock trailer or pickup truck to fit the wooden rails that were left behind. I couldn't afford to hire someone, so I looked around the farm to see what I could find. I immediately spotted my old 1998 Toyota Sienna minivan, still in good condition with 366,842 miles. Jim had recently returned it after he could afford to buy his first car.

This van travelled all over the country, from Williamsburg, Virginia to the Grand Canyon in Arizona. It climbed the peaks of the Rocky Mountains and took a ferry across Lake Huron. It hauled our camping gear to numerous state parks and took us to Great America each year. The van performed daily duties well, too, hauling our family to church, school, work, soccer games, the grocery store, and orthodontic appointments.

1998 Toyota Sienna minivan appears ready for farm duty.

Liz successfully passed her road test and got her driver's license with the van. When her first car died, a Cadillac with powder blue velvet seats that she bought for seventy-five dollars at a rummage sale, the van became her ride to school and work until her next car, a powder blue Honda, showed up. The van still contains a Zildjian sticker on the back window as a remembrance of hauling a drum set, cymbals, amps, and other performance gear to Jim's gigs over the years. When the kids went to college, the van went with them, and I finally got a different car.

Over the years, the van became known as "the beast" because of the very unique sound it made when we started it up or accelerated. The noise itself became a deterrent to talking on a cell phone while driving. John's girlfriend borrowed the van for a week when her newer car's transmission went out suddenly, and she joked later with Liz about the pleasure of driving the beast.

A Day on the Farm

Since my kids had graduated and gotten full-time jobs, they bought newer vehicles, and the Toyota Sienna minivan sat idle in the farm yard. I knew I could easily take out all the rear seats. I had performed that task hundreds of times, depending on where we were going, what we were hauling, and how many of my kids' friends joined us for the adventure. With the seats removed, the back looked quite spacious. I put a wooden panel from one of the lambing jugs behind the front seats and tied it tightly with twine just in case one of the sheep became curious about what I was doing up front.

Positioning the van to load up the animals became a little tricky because the back lift gate had to move straight up and back down again to close before I could pull away with the load, and I had to make sure it cleared the barn door. I practiced backing it down to the barn entrance and positioning hay bales between the van and the barn door. I then got a few portable wire panels and positioned them on each side of the bales. The system looked like it would work just fine.

Since I had never delivered livestock to the butcher before, I didn't know anything about what happened when they got there. I called to arrange a tour of the facility, and the owner and his wife were very cooperative. I figured I could fit five or six lambs in the back of the van, so I scheduled the first butcher date and called the first group of customers to let them know.

I backed up the van the night before and got everything in position. I moved the largest lambs to the pen closest to the door and went to bed early. The sun had just started rising when I went out to load them up. All the other animals called for food, so I quickly did the morning chores, and everyone settled down. This worked well because the lambs now expected their fresh supply of hay. I first opened the back of the van and then the door to the lamb pen. They all eagerly ran out. One of the lambs ran so eagerly that he knocked against one of the side panels and squeezed his way between the panel and the hay bale below. He escaped and started running outside the barn to an outdoor pen near some of the other sheep. *Oh, dear Lord,* I thought, *help me catch this lamb.*

I quickly closed the back gate of the van with the other four lambs safe inside. Fortunately, I could see the escaped lamb cornered by a fence, trying desperately to get through it to the other animals. I grabbed a halter and lead and went to retrieve the lamb. He resisted at first but realized he didn't have much of a choice and started cooperating. When I got to the van, I slid open the side panel door, and the lamb jumped right in when he saw his buddies again. By the time I pulled away from the farm, they were all happily munching on hay as we took a little ride through the country.

When we got to the butcher, a line of beautiful 4x4 pickup trucks with their fifteen- to twenty-foot livestock trailers waited to unload. I got in line with my trusty little minivan and the sheep in the back. The other equipment looked quite impressive, but when only one or two animals got out of each trailer, I thought maybe my transportation seemed a little more efficient. Granted, they all hauled cows and pigs, and I probably couldn't get a single large pig or steer in my van, but it worked just fine for me and the sheep. By the time I got to be third in line, I saw two young boys waiting on the cement entrance, drinking Mountain Dew. They looked about ten or eleven years old and were dressed in clean jeans and boots, plaid button-down shirts tucked in with belts, and little farm hats. I imagined what a special day this was for them to go along with Dad or Grandpa to take the animals that they helped raise to the butcher. As soon as they saw me pull closer with the minivan and the sheep in back, they pointed and started giggling. Everyone in line probably looked twice when they saw me, but I remained thankful that I made it safely with the cargo.

The first time I pulled up to unload, the young man who helped get the lambs out of the van looked a little surprised. But after a few trips, he was used to seeing me, and I felt like he was my friend, even though I didn't know his name. He was incredibly helpful to me and kind to my animals when they arrived. He led them to their little waiting pen with fresh water, and I headed for home. One time, when I pulled up in the rain, he told me that something was hanging from the bottom of the van, and sparks were flying from the metal dragging on the road. I took the van to the local mechanic the next day, and he got the broken piece removed in just a few minutes. Thank God the roads were wet that day.

I can barely fit five cull ewes in the back of the van when I have mutton orders, so sometimes only two or three go for a ride. Since they are flock animals, nobody goes alone. As much as I thought I would dread having to handle this task, it's not as bad as I thought it might be. Fortunately, I'm not a vegetarian. I know that my animals live very good lives, and then they travel happily through the countryside with their shepherd to their final destination. I couldn't hope for more.

Two cull ewes loaded and ready to take a ride in the country.

CHAPTER 12

Farm Lessons

I learned many things on the farm that I never thought I would need to know. Many of those tasks became critical to my survival, and I am very appreciative to everyone who shared their knowledge. Sometimes, though, farm lessons speak generally to life and serve as particularly important reminders about my life now.

The first lesson I learned was from Kira, the llama. Kira weighed about three hundred pounds, and she, like the other three llamas on the farm, lived with the sheep and alpacas to be a guardian. Coyotes surrounded the farm, and a friend who lived a few miles away had lost some of her sheep to coyotes. The lambs died a cruel death when a coyote showed up, and I wanted to protect my flock the best I could. When the llamas went out to pasture, they instinctively circled the perimeter to check things out. When they heard or saw a dog, they immediately approached it. Kira had a white spot on her black nose, and she loved to play in the water. She could be friendly and curious with people, and she would always put her feet in a stock tank when she got the chance. One summer, I taught her how to drink out of the water hose. She loved it. But she knew she had a job to do and was worth her weight in gold.

The first winter I spent alone on the farm, a rogue pit bull with a pink collar kept wandering over to the farm. I figured out where she belonged and talked to the owners twice about the dangers of letting her cross the highway alone. I witnessed cars slamming on the brakes to avoid hitting her, but she kept getting loose and making her way over to the farm. Soon she discovered that if she jumped against the sheep or alpaca pens and barked viciously, the animals became frantic. This excited her and concerned me greatly. Some of my customers witnessed her aggressive behavior and reported it to the sheriff's department. I prayed that the fences would hold and the pit bull couldn't get near enough to the animals to hurt them. One morning, when I returned from dropping my car off at the dealer to be serviced, I opened the door of the loaner vehicle to see the pit bull staring at me with a bloody face. I had only been gone twenty minutes, and when I looked toward the lambing barn, I could see Kira standing alone in the middle of the pen. I ran into the house to call 911, and the bloody pit bull followed me into the house. I grabbed the phone and ran back outside. The sheriff told me to check my animals, and he would be right over, along with the dog catcher.

I called my father-in-law, and he raced over to watch the store until the emergency ended. As I waited for the sheriff, I checked the ewes and their new lambs, and nobody seemed to have a scratch. The dog catcher soon arrived and retrieved the pit bull, who apparently made herself at home in my living room. When he came out with her, he said, "Looks like your dog beat her up pretty good." I told him I didn't have a dog at the time. I saw the pit bull's bloody, swollen eye and a gash on her jaw. I looked at Kira standing proudly and knew she did what she had to do to protect her flock. Kira's lesson: stand up to bullies, and protect your loved ones; do your job well when called on; and be sure to have some fun along the way.

Guard llamas Kira and Electra protect the flock of sheep in pasture.

The second lesson I learned came from Zella Mae, a beautiful black twin who got stuck in the pasture fence at least once or twice a week for about three months. Zella Mae repeatedly stuck her head through a hole in the wire netting to eat the grass on the other side of the fence. When she consumed the section in front of her, she stood there, calling for help, while the rest of the flock returned to the barn. Each time I walked down the lane or to the far end of the pasture, I just had to stand in front of her face, and she would back up, freeing herself from her dilemma. She then would run back to the barn to rejoin the flock. My friends mentioned to me several times that they would see a black sheep alone and stuck in the fence when they drove past the farm. It always turned out to be Zella Mae. Then I started getting text messages from people: "Looks like a sheep caught in the fence."

I responded, "Zella Mae again."

After a dozen times of walking down to Zella Mae caught in the fence, I just started calling out to her, "Back up, Zella Mae. The grass is *not* greener on the other side." She had no idea what I was saying, but as soon as she heard my voice, it startled her enough to take a step back and enjoy her freedom. It took a long time to see the simple truth behind her lesson: enjoy the good things that God gives you, and don't keep searching for something that separates you and keeps you stuck where you don't want to be.

Zella Mae learned that grass is not greener
on the other side of the fence.

The third lesson I learned was from Jim. He taught me how to drive the old Allis Chalmers tractor on the farm, which I didn't need to do very often, since Bob was quite versatile. He showed me which hole got water and antifreeze and which hole got diesel fuel. He rode along as I worked through the different gears. He then said, "You probably don't need to go above third gear for what you need to do, and don't ever connect the power take-off (PTO) unless someone is here to help you." I truly do enjoy the tractor ride in third gear, with the wind blowing through my hair, bouncing up and down in the old tractor seat. The lesson: you don't need more power than you can safely handle.

The fourth lesson came from Henry, the chicken. Kate called one day to ask if I would mind taking on a chicken at the farm. Her friend's grandson bought the baby chick at Easter from the local hardware store and became disinterested when the feathers started growing. Henry wasn't cute and fluffy anymore and ended up being raised in a dog crate in Grandma's house in the city. The chicken arrived with a large bag of feed and had free range of the farm. I agreed to keep the chicken as long as the feed lasted. I actually grew quite fond of Henry and started calling her Henrietta, since she wasn't a rooster. Henrietta clucked and cackled in the yard, in the sheep pen, and throughout the barns. She ate bugs, chased the farm cats when they got too close, and followed me around when I did chores. She let me pick her up and pet her; she was actually quite soft. But the bag of feed was getting empty, and Henrietta could barely waddle anymore.

Kate offered to let me use her ax to butcher the chicken, but I wasn't looking forward to what I had to do. Fortunately, the family that donated the Bibles to the store also raised chickens and invited me to bring Henrietta over on butchering day. I put Henrietta in a cat carrier and drove to their farm early in the morning before the fog burned off. The whole family helped me. They had a chicken plucking machine, and their thirteen-year-old daughter dressed and wrapped the bird for me. Henrietta weighed in at 10.4 pounds and went to feed a family through the local food pantry. Henry's lesson: always have an exit strategy.

CHAPTER 13

The Biggest Lesson

The Bible tells many stories about God turning evil into good. Even when people deliberately plotted deception and betrayal, God used their efforts for something amazing. Joseph's brothers mistreated him so horribly that they sold him into slavery only to see God put Joseph in a powerful position and save thousands of people from famine. God also used Joseph to demonstrate love, forgiveness, and compassion in the face of his family's cruelty toward him. Christ's enemies plotted His destruction, mocked Him, and crucified Him—but ultimately, this resulted in God's plan to save them from the sins they committed.

The world today is filled with evil that sometimes causes Christians to question God's plans. When I attended the Partners of Sex Addicts conference, some of the women were married to men who were leaders in their communities and church. One lady asked the first day, "How can God let these men cause so much suffering in His church?" God doesn't cause anybody to suffer. God is good. Satan is bad and clever. What better scheme could there be to get Christians to doubt their faith than to tempt with sexual misconduct in God's house? Sitting in a church pew on Sunday doesn't make a person a Christian any more than standing in a garage makes a person a car. We can't see into each church member's heart. Only God knows what's inside. Unfortunately, evil seeks to permeate Christ's church. We have to rely on God's truth to help us see that we cannot believe Satan's big lie. God doesn't create disease, hurt people, or make them suffer. That is a reflection of the evil in this world, designed by Satan and carried out by humans. We cannot always see the final result in God's plan.

My husband betrayed me beyond what I ever could have imagined. I found myself alone and vulnerable, desperately needing help and trusting God to send me people who could help. Most of the amazing people who came along were honest, compassionate, trustworthy, and highly skilled and generously offered their services. I am forever indebted to their kindness and look at them as human angels who reflect the face of Jesus in my life. Lots of good people abound in this world, and God answered my prayers by sending so many who showed up to help.

More people volunteered to help me who haven't even been mentioned here. They volunteered to do physically hard, dirty work, such as weeding in the garden or shoveling the manure out of the lambing barn by hand because machines can't fit through the doors. Ladies from the local Master Gardener's group volunteered to do landscaping and weeding. I didn't seek out these people; they came and offered to help out of the goodness of their hearts.

Another tremendous blessing God created out of this disaster was my friendship with Kate, whose betrayal from the cleric so similarly resembled mine. We understood each other's pain and fears, and we celebrated God's promises. Kate even came to help on the farm, getting dirty and sweaty from pulling weeds and then feeling muscles the next day she didn't know she had used. I attended the Bible study she led at church and have grown in my faith through the perspective she brought to God's Word. She truly is a sister in Christ. Toiling in the garden after the fall from sin has new meaning for her too when she presents lessons on Adam and Eve.

But my vulnerability also brought forth the human vultures. People came into my life pretending to be interested in helping me but truly seeking only their self-interest and personal needs. The first time it happened, I chalked it up to miscommunication over a verbal agreement. The chameleons eventually showed their true colors, and it became apparent they really didn't care about helping me but saw an opportunity to get something for themselves.

Some people showed up offering services they thought I wanted and needed because they had something they wanted *quid pro quo*. They seemed surprised that they couldn't convince me that their perception of my needs matched what they wanted to offer. I first needed to grieve from so many sudden losses in my life—my marriage, business partner, dog, mother-in-law, job, financial security, leisure time, and future dreams. Nobody walked through the door and offered to replace all of that, nor could they. I needed help, but I also sorely needed time to heal.

When someone showed up and offered to be my farmhand in exchange for renting my land for half of what I received the year before, I took notice. He presented himself as a Christian man and a leader in the community, so we drew up a five-page legal contract that spelled out the specific duties and when they needed to be done. I realize now that some people sign contracts with no care about or intention of fulfilling them. Or maybe they are just train wrecks waiting to happen, and I was going down the wrong track and got in the way. It's hard for me to see people at their worst. I want people to love God first and love their neighbors as themselves instead of believing that they can get ahead by loving only themselves and making sure their needs are met first.

Regardless of the motivations behind the actions, I found myself in a horrible situation that God turned around to be a tremendous blessing for me and the farm. I trusted God to help me make the payments on the farm, so I structured the rental contract to receive rent payments to coincide with the farm payment due dates. My banker actually suggested the strategy, and I liked the plan. When the first farmland rent payment came due, I didn't get paid. The renter had an excuse and brought the payment late. Then there was a problem with the check, and I couldn't wait another three weeks for it to clear the bank. My farm payment was due, and I didn't want to incur significant late fees and penalties.

I went to get the mail one day and found that my credit card company sent an envelope containing balance transfer checks with zero percent interest for more than a year. Here was a temporary solution, though humiliating and embarrassing for me to execute. I swallowed my pride. I quietly went to the bank to get more information about the renter's check problem and brought along the balance transfer check to make the farm payment. As I stood there at the counter, my banker spotted me. He came out of his office, walked across the lobby, and warmly greeted me. He asked me to stop in his office before I left to get caught up on how things were going on the farm.

We talked awhile, and he suggested that maybe I should consider selling some of the land. I didn't need 155 acres for the sheep, garden, and store operation and rented out a significant number of those acres. I certainly didn't need my income to be dependent on someone who didn't care whether I got paid or not. My banker referred me to a realty company that he knew dealt with farmland specifically, and I met with the Realtors the next day.

I prepared for the meeting with the Realtors by pulling out the appraisals, farm maps, and tax records. When they arrived, they asked to drive around the land to take a look. They came back, and I offered them the folder containing the records I gathered. They said they didn't need them yet and came up with a suggested listing price that was within a few thousand dollars of the appraisal. I signed the listing agreement and prayed that God would show me what to do. I knew that if God wanted me to keep all the land, no buyers would surface.

A Day on the Farm

Shortly after the For Sale sign went up, I had two full-price cash offers. My Realtor came to review the offers with me, and I selected the cleanest one. I didn't sign the offer immediately because I wanted to sleep on it, and we still had time before the deadline to respond. Within twenty-four hours, another party expressed interest. I had no idea that the northeast corner of the farm adjoined the neighboring city and its industrial park. Businesses were looking to relocate to the area, but the industrial park didn't have any available land. The city was now looking for land for economic expansion. Without knowing what offers were already on the table, the city offered above the listing price. I sold the vacant land for $580,000 and still have forty acres to farm, which seems adequate and more manageable.

Dealing with the renter through the entire rental period was a nightmare. He failed to complete most of the tasks listed on the contract, and I had to hire a neighbor to come and help get things done. But the land deal closed when the next farm payment came due. God used a horrible situation and turned it into a tremendous blessing for me, the city, and hundreds of people seeking employment with the new companies moving to the area.

The biggest lesson I learned through all of this is to trust God and His plan for my life. I can no longer doubt His goodness and mercy. He has shown me firsthand how He can take something meant for harm and turn into a blessing. His love endures forever.

CHAPTER 14

Forgiveness and Healing

Healing from trauma takes time, and each successive instance of trauma lengthens the process. But with God, nothing is impossible. The first step to healing is to end the trauma. A wound cannot heal if the scab is broken open again and again. You cannot heal from an abusive relationship if the abuse continues, and you cannot heal from betrayal and rebuild trust if the lies and deception continue unabated. I needed to end the trauma of a toxic relationship, as difficult as that would make my life. I knew I would suffer financial hardships. I knew I faced uncertainty and doubt. But I couldn't live a lie and pretend that my marriage was the way God intended. I desperately wanted peace in my life. I knew that God could restore my health and make me whole again, but I had to trust Him to work that out.

God showed me that the bitter roots of anger and resentment had to be destroyed in order to find inner peace. How is that possible? I studied His Word and read about forgiveness. We are commanded to forgive others as Christ forgave us. The command is simple and straightforward, but practicing forgiveness can be incredibly difficult. I needed to reach out for God's hand to guide me in the journey.

The profound example of God's love and mercy for us that He would send His only Son to suffer and die for our sins in order that we could be forgiven serves as a powerful model. But I could hardly fathom forgiveness in frigid weather as I froze doing daily chores. I could barely think about forgiveness when people blamed me for my husband's infidelity or told me what a horrible life I had. Forgiveness seemed far away when I looked at my bank statements. I could never find forgiveness as long as I focused on my pitiful circumstances. I needed to look more closely at God's model. His model wasn't rooted in hurt and pain; His model stemmed from pure love.

I prayed to forgive the people who hurt me, even if they didn't accept responsibility for what they did. I read Scripture and talked to my pastor. I learned that I can forgive people even if they are not sorry. Forgiveness is a process of releasing their debt to me, of letting go. Forgiveness is critical to being restored and made whole with God. Each day that I prayed the Lord's Prayer, the words stung when I got to the part about God forgiving our trespasses as we forgive those who trespass against us.

I then started looking at God's forgiveness of my sins. I had also hurt people and sinned. How could I expect God to forgive the horrible things that I did when I couldn't forgive those who hurt me? I prayed for help. I prayed for forgiveness of my unforgiving heart. I prayed for God to change my heart so that I could forgive. I desperately wanted and needed God's forgiveness, and I needed to forgive others.

When I least expected it, the cleric walked through the doors of the yarn shop and approached the counter. I was alone at the time, and he said, "This may be long overdue, but I want to apologize for destroying your marriage. Will you please forgive me?"

My heart said, "Yes, of course I forgive you." And those words came out of my mouth.

My husband apologized many times for hurting me. I know that was never his intention, because he never planned for me to ever find out. Even though he never disclosed everything he did during our marriage or accepted responsibility for some of the hurts he had caused, I finally reached a point where I could forgive him for everything. I told him I forgave him, and I have released him from all his debt.

As I healed, prayed, and asked God to show me what to do, He led me to be accountable for the hurts that I caused during our marriage. He showed me things that I did that were not God pleasing, and I made a list. I called my husband and went through each item on the page, saying how sorry I was for the things that I did. I asked him to forgive me, and I was blessed with his forgiveness. I stated emphatically that I was not responsible in any way for his infidelity and betrayal during our marriage and explained that God had shown me the truth of that statement. That sin was between him and God, who knows all our sins, even our secret sins. He agreed. I asked if there were any hurts that I caused that weren't on my list, and he couldn't think of any. I wished him well and told him that I would continue to pray for his healing as well as mine. I hung up the phone and thanked God for bringing me to my knees and showing me what forgiveness truly means.

The healing continues. I started writing down my blessings and thanking God for His goodness in my life. I recently added peace and joy to the list. In time, I know that I will thank Him for restoring my health and wholeness completely.

EPILOGUE

Early in my career, before I married and had children, I applied for a position within the company where I worked. I knew my qualifications matched what the job required, and the interview went very well. I almost celebrated the promotion before I found out that the manager hired an outside candidate with less experience. Devastated, I went home and cried about the injustice to my roommate, God, and just about anyone who would listen. I ended up leaving the company and taking a temporary job at a larger corporation. Within three months, I was hired permanently in a position that changed my entire career trajectory. The job paid significantly more than the position I didn't get, and I traveled internationally in the new job. I formed friendships that have lasted a lifetime. As I look back, I see God's hand in all of it. He knew the perfect job waited for me.

I share this story and others like it with my children when they experience disappointments. God has a plan; we just don't know what it is yet. I continue to pray, and as I get older, I can see how God answers my prayers. Many times, I don't get exactly what I ask for.

Recently, I prayed for a dog to help herd the sheep. Liz researched some breeds and suggested looking at a Bouvier des Flandres. I contacted some breeders, and one of them sent me a video of her dogs, including how they helped with her sheep and goats. I arranged to get a puppy. When Mickayla arrived at two months of age, she met the lambs and spent time with me and the animals. She met people in the store, went to puppy class, learned some basic obedience, and grew. As a young puppy, she even barked in the middle of the night to let me know that a lamb had jumped the pen and needed help. By six months of age, she had no interest in the sheep except to try to get one off to the side to play with her. Ironically, the sheep have rarely escaped their pastures since she arrived, and Jim modified all the fencing. I now call her Mickie, and she is a very friendly, loving dog who apparently got bypassed with the herding gene.

But that's how God works. I prayed for a dog to herd the sheep, and He gave me a loyal companion who would guard me with her life.

When I first found myself alone on the farm, I prayed for courage, strength, and confidence. God filled me with the Holy Spirit. I prayed for love and acceptance. God showed me the face of Jesus.

Sometimes our prayers aren't answered the way we want. Because God loves His children so much, He chooses to bless us and give us much more than we ask. He doesn't always give us what we want; He gives us what we need.

I prayed for unfailing faith and hope for the future, and God gave me a farm.

Printed in the United States
By Bookmasters